THROUGH A STONE WALL

LESSONS FROM THIRTY YEARS OF WRITING

by

Ardath Mayhar

The Borgo Press
An Imprint of Wildside Press

MMVIII

*I.O. Evans Studies in the Philosophy
and Criticism of Literature*
ISSN 0271-9061

Number Forty

SECOND EDITION

CONTENTS

FOREWORD

This small collection of essays was written over a period of a number of years, in connection with the classes in fiction writing that I have taught from time to time.

While they may overlap, to some extent, material to be found in the many books on writing on the shelves, I believe that there is enough hard-won experience reflected here to justify another volume in this field.

There are many pitfalls in the business of writing. Any professional has had numbers of experiences that can be of help to those engaged in trying to write for publication. I have tried to put up signs, here and there:

DO NOT ENTER—
THERE ARE ALLIGATORS IN THIS SWAMP

BEWARE—VICIOUS PUBLISHER

ENTER AT YOUR OWN RISK

but also:

COME ON IN—THE WATER'S FINE!

INTRODUCTION TO THE SECOND EDITION

Although this book was written a number of years ago, and for that reason some of the material included is outdated, the basic principles here are those I consider necessary if you are to write engaging and involving fiction. Creating characters that become real to the reader, plots that offer interest, dramatic impact, and challenge, and contexts that are either new to the reader or are familiar, yet which also are described in such fresh and unusual terms that you see them anew—those are the flesh and bones of fiction.

—Ardath Mayhar
Chireno, Texas
September 2006

CHAPTER ONE

DISPATCH FROM THE FRONT: NEVER WASTE ANYTHING

For twenty years I have advised my writing students never to waste anything that happens to them, be it pleasant or painful. I thought I had taken that advice as far as it could go on my own, but, as life has a habit of doing, I learned that I hadn't even begun.

In September 1999 I lost my husband of forty-one years. He had been terribly ill for many years, but I learned then that sometimes death is a friend, not something to grieve over. In October I swerved to miss a small animal in the road, lost control, and wrecked my car. That was when fresh material began to pour in, uninvited, unwanted, but hopefully not to remain unused.

I know how it feels to be that guy bound solidly to a back-board, staring at the roof of the ambulance while EMTs work on you. (Note: They bind your head down so tightly that it feels as if a quarter-sized bit at the back of the skull is slowly turning into mush.) I understand what it feels like to wait, still bound to the board, while the ER team assesses the injuries and waits for an opening in X-ray to make sure just what all you broke. I did a pretty good job on myself, too: fractured ankle that needed surgery to put the jigsaw puzzle back together, using six screws and a plate, plus a compression fracture in the spine at T-5, which is just where the lungs work hardest in breathing.

The term "Guarded Breathing" meant nothing to me before. Now I understand. This means that the pain is so intense that your lungs refuse to expand more than the minimum amount needed to supply oxygen. You breathe in short gasps, which makes eating all but impossible.

When that term was used on a rerun of the old *Emergency* show a while back, I understood exactly what the victim was feeling.

Now if I can only get it onto paper in a story, this experience will prove valuable. Waste nothing, remember?

Have you heard about pain management special-ists? Bless them all! One came to my rescue after the ankle surgery and did a Thoracic Epidural, in-jecting a cocktail of drugs directly into the com-pressed disk. IT STOPPED HURTING, compara-tively speaking. I intend to use this rather new medical discipline in a story or book, before I am too old to attack the computer. In addition, I can sympathize with anyone wearing a plastic back brace and describe its man-eating habits. This thing encased my entire torso, though the bosom could have contained at least one more woman of my di-mensions. If I could sing, I could have stood in for a Wagnerian soprano. I carried my purse, a book, etc.

in it when going to the doctor, as using what I have been given is an old habit.

I suspect the slug from a .350 Magnum wouldn't penetrate the thing, and I could have fallen off the roof without reinjuring my back, I feel certain. Never again will I turn a turtle onto its back, for now I understand the helplessness such a big, thick shell entails.

Going to the bathroom and getting out again while wearing it was simply impossible. My sister and her husband took me home from the hospital to recuperate and put me in their room, by day when they were at work, so I could get to their small bathroom, using the walker. The first time, I went wearing Matilda, the brace, I sat down without a problem. Though my brother-in-law had installed a bar to grab, my arm motion was so curtailed and my leg so unstable that when I tried to pull myself up again it didn't help.

The space was too narrow to get my elbows down so I could undo the six Velcro straps that held Matilda on. Luckily my sister came home for lunch and freed me from the trap. This was no situation for a long-time claustrophobe!

Speaking of Velcro—I now know how it might feel to wrestle an octopus. Using the wheelchair, I went to the bathroom (the larger one) but shed Matilda after entering.

When I was ready to leave, I decided to save my sister some effort by taking the brace back to the bedroom with me; I picked it up.

Those straps grabbed everything—pants legs, hair, skin, cast—until I threw it away in desperation and fled as fast as I could wheel my chair.

When I got into a walking cast, it, too, had a set of Velcro straps. Getting caught between Matilda and the walking cast was something like being in the middle of a fight between King Kong and Godzilla.

Emancipation from Matilda gave me a bit of insight into what it would feel like to be let out of a straitjacket. Getting out of the cast was almost as satisfying. I thought I was on the road to recovery at full speed.

Then I discovered I had a staph infection, as often happens after surgery. I learned, to my utter disgust and despair, what fragility feels like. Having been strong (East Texas dairy farmers have to be that) and active all my life, being incapacitated, not to mention WEAK, was a revelation and gave me a lot of material that may prove useful, given time. A lot of time. Some things have to "cool off" quite a bit before you can bear to go back into them in depth.

Now, five months after the accident, I am truly recovering and can walk without a cane. The back, having been abused to its limit while I was dairying, got better on its own without surgery, and my spirits are good. Being an incurable optimist helps there.

I turned seventy in February, and my doctors, all the way, have been boggled at the way I heal. One of the neurologists came into my hospital room in the middle of the second night and asked me to squeeze his hands as hard as I could.

Never assume that an old woman lying flat on her back is weak. Remember that I milked cows for ten years and a goat after that.

I squeezed, and he flinched, said, "That is enough of that!" and retreated.

In March I attended AggieCon, a science fiction convention at Texas A&M, driving myself there and back. I walked up and down stairs as if the ankle was completely well (it isn't quite, but getting there).

After being unable to write for almost three years, drained by my husband's illness as well as keeping our bookshop afloat without help, I can now sit down at the computer and START SOME-THING NEW without wanting to scream and run. The con recharged my batteries.

The most valuable thing I have learned is that a positive attitude will carry you through almost anything. You can make stories out of the strangest and most painful things, if you remember them. I made mental notes all the way along, and I intend to use them all before I sink forward, dead, with my nose in the keyboard.

CHAPTER TWO

THE LEAD PARAGRAPH

In today's overworked and understaffed publishing world, it is more and more true that the decision to read or not to read a manuscript may depend upon the beginning of the story or nonfiction piece. Editors read huge stacks of manuscript every week, and their eyeball-power is strained to its limits.

It is not, however, only the editor who makes his decision on the basis of two or three pages. The casual reader, browsing through a bookstore, will more often than not decide upon the purchase of a book by reading the first paragraph.

I have done this myself, knowing that some books take a hundred pages to hit their strides. And yet my eyes, too, suffer from overwork, and this is such a convenient shortcut.

As one who has taught people writing, as well as editing the work of beginning and professional writers, I can say with some truth that you usually know at the end of that first paragraph whether the work is going to be worth the time and eyestrain devoted to completing it. By the third page, you can be sure that if there will be any strengths they would have showed up.

But the first page and the first paragraph and the first LINE of the first paragraph can grab you so solidly, in some cases, that you are well and truly caught by the proverbial Narrative Hook. Never discount its value.

This is not a device used by hacks to sell potboilers, believe me. It is a necessary concomitant of writing commercially viable prose, and it is as true for nonfiction writers as it is for those who create fiction.

Many years ago I attended a writer's conference at which one of the prominent agents of the day was a speaker. I will never forget the line that he quoted as hooking him on a story that turned out to be disappointing, yet which he read to the end, simply because of the lead.

"They piled out of the cabin and squared off in the snow." That line has stuck in my mind since 1952, if you can believe that. Look at it—how lean, and yet how full of information it is!

You are in the north country (cabin and snow). At least two people are involved in the action, and there is a fierce altercation in progress, or they wouldn't be serious enough to carry the action out into the snow. In twelve words, a novice writer stumbled upon the perfect way to begin a story that he had not yet learned the skill to complete on the same level.

Another fine example of a lead line that pulls you, willy or nilly, into the story is that of Mary Renault's novel *The Last of the Wine*. It is to the effect that when the narrator is depressed about anything, he recalls that "On the day I was born my father wanted me killed." This jerks you up short and will not let you go until you learn all the circumstances surrounding this character and his background.

Once you have that perfect first line, you cannot afford to let your fishing line go slack. The paragraph into which it leads should develop that initial statement, creating still more interest, suspense, or atmosphere.

It is a good idea to analyze books and stories that you particularly enjoy. Watch how the writer went about catching your attention. How did he introduce his story? How was the main character introduced? What background is indicated, either directly or by implication, and what effect does it have upon your perception of the action and the people involved?

There are many ways in which to begin a story, and new ones are being invented all the time. Yet every story has its own best beginning, and it is up to you as the writer to learn how to find it, and, indeed, at which point it is best to start telling your tale. Not only will this affect the reception of the story, it will color your own approach to writing it, for that beginning is also your own first immersion in this story you want to tell.

There have been stories that had problems that were solved when the writer went back and created a new lead. I have seen entire books rewritten in first instead of third person, or vice-versa, as a result of restudying that lead. To a great extent, it is even more important than the ending.

Actually, by the time a reader gets to the end of the book, he has usually bought it and can't do anything about it, so a disappointment there creates only a delayed problem.

An editor can usually spot a problem with an ending and make excellent suggestions for correcting it. But if your lead paragraph hasn't snagged that editor into buying the book, you will never know.

CHAPTER THREE

ENDINGS

If your lead paragraph is an inducement to the reader/editor to finish reading your story, then the last few sentences can be your opportunity to make him glad that he did. It is so easy to get lazy near the end of a book or a story.

You have worked very hard, forming good characters and a fascinating plot. You have done a wonderfully dramatic climax. At this point you are just finishing up, it sometimes seems, and your task is done.

But it isn't.

At this point, you need to provide some sort of summation of your story. Have you settled all the important situations? Have you tied off all the subtle threads that spun off from the main plotline? Perhaps all your characters are now prepared to live happily ever after, but something still remains to be done.

You have to make it all make sense. Something needs to convince the reader that all the *sturm und drang* was worthwhile, that the characters and the reader and even the writer learned something or accomplished something, even if it was only enjoyment.

It is at this point that you make a lasting friend and reader. Here you convince him that you are a writer after his own heart, one who takes infinite pains to make certain that his sense of fitness and completion is satisfied. You have hung in there to the very end, trying hard all the while.

How many stories have you read that left you with a vague sense that you were uncomfortable with their endings, no matter how logical they might seem? Something was simply amiss. You couldn't say just what, but something was.

If you react as I do, you seldom pick up another work by that particular writer, just because of that one reaction.

It is like an itch you can't scratch or a pebble in your shoe. It isn't vitally important, but it isn't something you intend to repeat unnecessarily, either.

At the end, the last thread must be tied, and some final statement needs to pull the whole story together into a coherent whole. As an example, I will use the last couple of paragraphs from my first published novel, *How the Gods Wove in Kyrannon* (Doubleday, 1979):

> But we shall be, ever and always, alert to the outside world. Never again will I shut myself away to save my own hurt. Linked into the skein of spirits that have wrought together in the name of the gods, we shall know what passes overmountain. Should another seek to

take the Tyrant's place, he will find himself beset from south, from west, from north, by forces of terrible power. We go not to be hermits but free beings, living as we love to live.

So the pattern is completed, the shuttles return to their places, and the hands of the gods lie idle, or turn to other tasks.

CHAPTER FOUR

BASIC NEEDS

There are a number of elements that can make your life as a writer much easier, if you know about them from the beginning, instead of having to stumble into them by accident as you stagger through the creative maze. I will list here some of the things I have learned by hard experience:

1. Read widely, not only in the field in which you are interested, but also in many different areas, from children's books to classics, from science fiction to mysteries. I also suggest strongly that any writer read psychology, anthropology, archeology, and ancient history, getting some idea of the multitudes of ways in which our kind has lived, what cultures have existed, and how our minds work. A deep understanding of mankind and why he is as he is will give every character you ever write about much more reality than you would believe possible.

2. Don't pay too much attention to books and courses that teach you how to write (including this one). They can be helpful, useful, and they can save you a lot of bumbling around in the dark, but every writer has his own best way in which to approach

his craft. Don't let anyone tell you, "This MUST be done in this manner," or "Nobody works that way!" Believe me, there isn't a way in which somebody doesn't work successfully.

3. Study the English language. This is your bag of tools, your element, and an understanding of its grammatical construction is a powerful ally. But in addition, savor the words you have at your command. As you read work you admire, study the ways in which the author uses words to express his meaning in a unique manner. Read poetry to learn how to add rhythm and depth to your writing by the uses of unusual nouns and verbs. Think in unusual terms. And if it lies within your capacities at all, learn to spell!

4. Don't misunderstand the old adage, "Write what you know." This doesn't really mean never to write about anything you haven't experienced or observed. That would mean that nobody would ever write creatively at all, simply reporting what came within his/her purview. No, this means that if you write about an alien world, SEE that world inside your mind. Visualize the things that you write about, learn to know all about the places as well as the people with whom you tenant your tales. If you do write about the sorts of things you see from your kitchen window, do it in unusual terms, with original insights. You can make poetic or philosophical conclusions arise from the most mundane situations, if you understand how to look at them with the creative eye.

5. Learn the techniques of writing and then follow your instincts. Rules are made to be broken— but know the rule and break it intentionally, not ac-

cidentally. If you use a technique that defies the canon, and it means arguments with editors and copyeditors, even if it means loss of a sale, if it works for you and you know it will work for readers, stick to your guns. It is the writing that is your reward. For money, you should have become a plumber.

6. Don't rewrite just to be rewriting, because you have read that writers MUST. A good rule of thumb is to do one draught as well as you possibly can, and then go back for a second that is BETTER. Any third and fourth and fifth draught writing labels you either sloppy or afraid to finish and measure your work against the market. Use your critical judgment, after the work has had a few weeks to cool off. Or get a knowledgeable acquaintance to read it for flow and coherence. It is possible to omit something really vital, simply because you know it so well that you think you have it down...and you don't. People who work for thirty years polishing a novel have other jobs that support their dependents.

7. Do your best to keep in touch with other writers, if only by mail. This is a lonely field, and even the most devoted and understanding spouse doesn't really understand how you feel when something you know is good gets rejected by all the suitable markets in existence. Another writer, with whom you can share triumph and frustration, can keep you writing.

8. Don't be discouraged by rejection. Remember that it is this specific piece of writing, not you as a human being, that is being rejected. And don't rewrite every time your brainchild comes home from the wars. If two or three editors mention the same

apparent flaw, it's time to look at that element of the story/article/book and reassess its clarity. If you begin to see loose spots and ragged edges, after a time, that, not earlier, is the time to begin a rewrite. Principally, selling is a matter of sending the same piece out and out and out until it sells. When you have used up all the good markets, put the work in a file cabinet for a couple of years and then start the process all over again. Editors change with remarkable regularity, and you can hit an entirely new batch after a reasonable lapse of time. Upon resubmitting, however, it is a good idea to change the title, for companies sometimes keep logs of manuscripts coming and going.

9. Don't be sidetracked by literary fads. The sort of writing that lasts is that which finds a response in people who are neither academics, writers, nor critics. Writing is for people, not for those who practice artistic one-upmanship or academic obscurantism. Any mode undecipherable to anyone except a professor of creative writing or another avant-garde writer is going to die soon and completely. Modern fads do not last.

10. WRITE! After work. While the washer runs, during fire drills, while driving or sitting in the dentist's office or the bathroom. Write in your mind if you don't have a pencil and paper. Make notes of every person you find interesting, every place you live or visit, all the odd facts you come across. Retain flavors and scents and the feel of specific places. Everything you have ever known is going to come in handy to you as a writer, so write! And write! And write! Too few professions have any inherent joy, nowadays. Ours is one that includes skill

and love and reality and imagination. We have something inside us that we must put onto paper, in order to communicate it to our fellow human beings. We live with the demanding and frustrating elements of the business, simply because we love what we do.

CHAPTER FIVE

CREATING ATMOSPHERE

Styles for creating the moods and atmospheres of stories have changed drastically, over the years. Things that worked for Dickens or Poe, Lovecraft, or William Morris are not what modern editors are looking for. Poe himself, reborn into our present, would have to write in the modern idiom in order to sell his work. The overload of adjectives and adverbs is no longer acceptable to modern taste, although the creation of atmosphere and mood is vital to many sorts of stories.

Horror comes to mind at once, and many sorts of suspense and romantic fiction, as well as that for children. Many kinds of stories depend for their effect upon the masterful creation of their particularly necessary moods.

No longer can we line up an array of verbiage and expect it to do our work for us. Instead of ranks of adjectives, we have to find compelling nouns and strong and unusual verbs to help us create the effect we need and want.

Consider the contrast in two versions of the following sentence:

It was a gray, damp, depressing day. And then: *It was a foul day, gray with damp.* Doesn't the second have more real feeling in it of the mood of that day?

I am often asked by my students, "What do you mean by strong nouns and verbs?"

Well, first of all, I do not mean just nouns and verbs. A house is just a house. But a cottage is one specific sort, a fortress is another, and a bungalow still another. Each carries with it a set of connotations that might help to set up a story.

People, too, have their own archetypes that can be shown by unusual nouns: He was a monster of ingratitude. She was a battleaxe. They were more a coven than a family. He seemed to be a kind of Visigoth, lost in an era in which he didn't belong. All these tell a great deal about the people described, without the use of any adjective at all.

Verbs are just as flexible and expressive. He lunged. She exploded with rage. We darted across the rainy street. The dog menaced the intruder. These are not terms that you use in everyday conversation, but they work beautifully within a story.

Of course, atmosphere can be created in many ways. Mark Twain said once that any writer is entitled to a single spell of weather in his career, because most do it so badly. I really don't agree with that, for weather can help to create a mood and atmosphere with great felicity.

In order to use weather in this way, you need a long and attentive acquaintance with the natural world. You need to know how it feels to walk or to work in a thunderstorm. How it sounds and feels to walk on snow. You need to know how it sounds when a forest bows before a strong gust of wind. Weather is a constant in our lives, and if we take note of it in all its aspects, we can use it to good effect.

Houses, too, can have a strong effect upon people. A certain house can create a mood or arouse expectations in your characters and your readers. New houses smell of paint and fresh wood. They feel unused, fresh, as if they were waiting for things to happen inside their walls.

Old houses have a lot more atmosphere. They pop and creak, shelter small creatures that spin webs or nibble wires or burrow up through the wood of their frames. They smell like mold and mildew, furniture polish and mice and years and years of meals. You can do a great deal to set up your story just by using the place in which you set it.

Just for example, I will spin off a scene here that may help to demonstrate what I mean:

The door opened upon a hall so narrow that I wondered how they ever brought Uncle Ben's coffin through it without scraping off the pallbearers on either side. The place still smelled of funeral flowers, but it smelled more strongly of Aunt Jane's cooking. Hot vegetable soup, cornmeal muffins, frying chicken, huge pot roasts...all those still lingered like ghosts, penetrating the very paper of the walls and the finish of the furniture.

It had probably been that very cookery, the pride of all Aunt Jane's family for generations, that had taken Uncle Ben to such an early grave, I was thinking, as I closed the door behind me and stood listening to the subtle cricks and cracks the old house was always muttering to itself. The level of its complaint rose as Aunt Jane came back down the stairs, her hat off and her good dress laid aside. It was time to cook again, no matter how many casseroles and cakes neighbors and friends had left in the kitchen.

At this point, I might well go ahead and write a story that begins with this scene...it intrigues even me. It could be horror or a mainstream family story or a juvenile or suspense. And yet the atmosphere in that hallway would color every aspect of the plot.

While atmosphere does not move your story, *per se*, it can supply the textured background against which your actors will play out their parts. It is a skill well worth cultivating.

CHAPTER SIX

MAKING THINGS HAPPEN

In order to write action that grips the reader and makes him live the thing that is happening in the story, you have to learn to write about action as if you were involved in it yourself. That is the only way, for someone who stands off at a distance and describes what is going on is going to lose his reader's interest very quickly.

The method I have found that works best for me is really very similar to method acting. I go inside the protagonist most involved in the scene, and then I act and react within his skin, feeling his emotions and pains and triumphs. See the contrast between the following scenes:

> John walked into the garden. It was cold, and he shivered as he hid behind a bush and waited to hear the signal. The danger that faced him was very real, and he might not come out of this formal garden alive, he knew quite well.

28

Now how about this:

> John waited for a moment, listening for any sound in the chill formality of the garden. The wind, catching his coat collar, made his earlobes ache, as he found a hidden spot behind a camellia bush, now frost-touched and stiff, and settled to wait. He wondered when the signal would come...and if he would survive this contact and return tonight to Jennifer's warm room and comforting presence.

Watch what happened there. I went into that garden with him. I felt that gust of wind. I heard the camellia bush rustle. I longed, with him, for the warmth of his girl and the safety of her room, and I dreaded, with him, the signal that would take him out into danger.

This is not a difficult thing to learn to do. And once you do learn it, the very act of becoming your character will provide a great deal of detail, of emotion, of inner depth that otherwise you would never know was there. And now let's see what happened to John, there in that garden.

> The whistle, when it came, was shrill and hurt his ears. He sighed and straightened, still cautious, to peer from behind his bush. Even as he moved to leave its shelter, hard hands caught at him from the other side of the low hedge.

"Got him!" said a strangled voice. "Here, haul him over!"

He felt the stiff twigs of the hedge scraping his skin, tearing along the rough weave of his trousers and coat, as he was jerked unceremoniously from his position to the other side of the stubbly growth. He went limply, as if caught off guard, but when his feet touched the ground, he exploded like some delayed action bomb. His right fist sank into an unprotected belly, as his left hand tangled in a beard and yanked a face down to meet his lowered skull. A nose broke audibly against his head. His feet were busy, too, and a suppressed shriek told him he had connected with someone's groin. He heaved backward, away from the now less enthusiastic hands, and in an instant he was over the hedge again and out of the garden, leaving whoever had betrayed him to sort out the catastrophe without him.

You have to get into that fight yourself. You have to know something about hurting and being hurt in a hand-to-hand situation. Having a younger brother, as I did, helped me with that a great deal.

You have to choreograph the action so that you won't have someone doing something physically impossible or going in two directions at once, or simply going about what he's doing all wrong. That will lose you a reader in a hurry.

A battle that is described in fiction must be handled in much the same way. You need to figure out just what parts of it are crucial to your story. You need to put one or more characters into important engagements and then to follow them through their parts, linking each together by transition or 'reports' in order to make the shape of the battle conform to your needs.

The difference between this technique and the long distance one can be seen if you will read any history textbook account of an historic battle and then will go and find personal accounts of that same battle, such as those that Bruce Catton used in his wonderful Civil War books. The difference between the immediate and personal and the distant and impersonal is the difference between the interesting and the dull.

An important part of action, as well as every other aspect of a story, is the feelings that the characters have and that the reader finds affecting him. A person with no emotions is not a real one, and you must, as with the action writing, make the characters' emotions your own.

Grief, anger, fear, pleasure, triumph, joy, anticipation—all the range of human emotional response is at your command. Few writers, or anyone else, can go through a life without knowing all those and more. Take your own feelings and pour them into your characters. You will get a surprise. Your crotchety old grandfather character will not deal with sudden anger in the same way that his fearful young granddaughter will. Suddenly, your own feelings will assume a wide range of differences, each suitable to the person who is involved in the emotional situation.

Make your reader feel for and with the characters.

Watch:

> She sat, limp and unmoving, on the shore, staring out at the spot where her child had gone down. Tears had not come.
>
> Grief had not come...not yet.
>
> She felt drained, exhausted, cold as the bare-branched oak trees that leaned over the river. It would have been such a relief to cry, to shout, to rage at God and nature and her own weakness, and yet she could not.
>
> She felt as if cold mud filled her, throat to belly, and she would never move or speak again. One huge pain, she would sit here in the damp forever, staring at the water that had taken her son.

And now for another:

> Clarence almost danced along the stone-flagged walk. His black-gloved fingers grasped the gift tightly, and he had to loose them consciously, for fear of crushing the delicate filigree of the brooch.
>
> Cynthia would be so delighted, so proud—she would know that he had

saved for a year to buy this special gift, and she would, perhaps, smile that wide, warm smile that welcomed him home to more than four walls and a dinner.

It is useful to write small exercises like the ones above, just to hone your ability to evoke action and emotion, not to mention imagery and characterization. A pianist or a violinist must practice. There is not a thing wrong with a writer's taking a leaf from the musicians' book and practicing, as well.

CHAPTER SEVEN

CHARACTERIZATION

For one who is just beginning to write, sometimes a character chart can be of great help, before he ever begins writing the story at all. It would go something like this:

Name, age, and sex
Background (education, parents and siblings)
Present circumstances (job, or whatever, marital status, emotional condition, health)
Personal habits and preferences
Personality traits (including any psychological problems or hang-ups, as well as strengths)
Response to change or stress
Ambitions and dreams

Most of this will never even be mentioned in the story you write about this person, but the fact that you have taken the trouble to find out what makes him tick will help you to make him breathe, as well.

Few stories succeed that are not written around some memorable character, be it an admirable or a despicable one.

Building such a fictional person is not easy, and many techniques have been devised for making it become possible. Technique, however, cannot substitute for personal observation...the sort of mental note-taking that writers do even under the most distressing or painful or comical circumstances. You need to cultivate the habit of noticing with all your might. This is the most vital tool in your kit, alongside remembering what you observe.

We all live among people, work with them, talk with them almost every day of our lives. Every facet of the interesting ones remains with us, filed someplace deep inside, and you can depend upon your own personal "computer" to correlate the traits you have collected, the aspects that have roused your interest. It will tidily conjure up, when you need a character, a person who seems quite real but is not exactly like anyone you ever met. It will be a composite of many, with a dollop of something else that is your own intuition added to the mix.

You want your reader to look up from your story and say, "Why I know somebody exactly like that!" That is the accolade.

Once you have some experience at writing and characterizing, you can just wing it, when it comes to those who inhabit your tales. You can start a story and have your character come walking up a road or out of a house to introduce him/herself to you. You tag along after, sharing the adventures and experiences of these people.

That is a lot of fun, and you can truly astonish yourself with the things you can learn about this stranger as you watch him at his work or play. As you write, you learn more and more about his habits, prejudices, attitudes, and preoccupations, just as you do with real people you meet in life.

Often, as you near the end of a story, you will find something new and startling that will make you need to return to the beginning to add a clue, so unexpected aspects of personality of experience will not come as a shock to your reader. This is what rewrites are for, and that is when you catch up such loose ends and knot them neatly.

There will come a time, as you gain experience and expertise, when you will find yourself laying in your clues as you go along, without even realizing what you are doing. When you reach a pivotal point, you will look back at what you have been doing all along and say to yourself, "Why THAT is what that was all about!"

If that sounds strange, just recall that writers are rather strange people, whose subconscious minds are more esoteric than most.

I find that too many beginning writers tend to itemize their characters, rather than to make them reveal themselves to the reader. "She had long blond hair, blue eyes, and a slender figure made for modeling bikinis."

This sounds more like an inventory. Not too bad, but the same information can be given much more entertainingly and revealingly, as well. Forward the plot if you can!

> She stood on the shore, long blond hair streaming on the breeze. Her eyes were almost the blue of the sea across which she was gazing. The young man who was swimming in with the tum-

bling breakers noted with appreciation that she had the kind of figure made for modeling a bikini.

Now you have set up a context, a possible plot, and you have also described your heroine instead of taking inventory of her attributes. You have some flavor and atmosphere, as well.

Sometimes a character walks into your tale and takes over. Most writers who have been at it a while have had to rewrite whole books in order to create a plotline for a late arrival who proves to be as important and interesting as the protagonist.

Never waste this kind of personality. Usually, the story will be greatly improved, no matter how much rewrite is required, by the presence of this vigorous intruder. A character who is treated like a pawn in a chess game usually has all the personality of a pawn, as well.

The takeover sort of fictional person carries a story, quite often, in a direction you had no intention of taking. Outlines are all very well, if you want to plot a book in cold blood, but I would hesitate forever before hewing to an outline instead of giving such a character his head and letting him take off toward his own destiny. When this happens, pant along behind, typing as fast as you can, and hope that the action won't get too fast to report.

CHAPTER EIGHT

MAKING NONFICTIONAL CHARACTERS COME TO LIFE

When writing about real people, your approach to making your characters seem three-dimensional, breathing human beings is not entirely different from that you use when making fictional characters. Living people, however, already have their histories on record, perhaps friends, relatives or acquaintances who can remember things about them, if they happen to be no longer among the living.

This saves some invention, for which you substitute research. A living person can usually be approached for an interview. There is nothing like speaking directly to your subject, hearing his voice, watching his expressions, reading his body language, to help you to make him come to life on paper.

Never believe that simply because you are dealing with fact you do not need to make this person believable. Fictional techniques make for much more gripping and intriguing nonfiction.

While it is harder to find the reality of a living human being than it is for one you have created from scratch, it can be done. Effort, time, research, and care help to make this come about, as is evident from some of the brilliant work of the best journalists and historians.

Find all the facts that fit into that character outline I gave earlier. Fill in everything else discoverable about your protagonist. And then make that person begin to breathe upon the page.

CHAPTER NINE

THE SHAPING OF LANGUAGE

"Let it roll trippingly off the tongue," said Hamlet.

Yet the effect of the words thus rolled can be astoundingly different, even through spoken with the same intonations and in the same phrasing. A flat Texas drawl, a Vermont twang, a Mississippi softness, an Ohio sharpness will all alter the impact of the same statement. Only spoken in a fair imitation of the original British precision can Shakespeare be truly Shakespeare.

How much more difference can be seen when each of those accents tells a story—even the same one—in its own vernacular, using its own set of colloquialisms and its own native rhythms. Turns of speech quite common in one area of the same country can seem completely alien or indecipherable in another.

Even more noticeable is the difference of speech derived from different linguistic backgrounds. Listen to some one of Italian origin talk with one from a Hebrew-speaking family. Ignore the meaning of the conversation, just listen to the sounds and the rhythms of the talk. Without seeing either speaker, you will recognize immediately which is which.

Every language imprints its own style on those reared using it. The grammar of every tongue differs, in some respects, from all others, even those with the same parent-language. Accents fall here, not there. Verbs go here, not there. When one learns a foreign language, he uses it according to his old patterns of speech, unless he painstakingly works to remove all trace of his accent of origin.

Grammar is different from tongue to tongue. Latin, for instance, places the verb at the end of the clause or the sentence. If you translate literally such a line as *Femina pulchra est*, you will come out with "Woman beautiful she is," which would give your speech a strange twist until you learned the English construction.

The structure of language can be seen to have a strong impact not only on the pronunciation but the basic grammatical structure of English as it is spoken by those who learned it in adulthood. The phonetic attributes of language shape the movements of the tongue, lips, and throat, and they stamp their mold upon the learned language, which forms what we call accent.

There is another function, however. The word shapes the thought, to a remarkable extent. A language lacking a wide range of abstractions will produce little philosophy. One without precise mathematical terms may produce few physicists or theoretical mathematicians. A language dealing strictly with the practical here and now, with no patience or scope for the poetic, will tend to produce pragmatic people as well as frustrated ones who might have been poets in another culture. Yet language is a function of people, and they expand their tongue to fit their needs in any living society. It may borrow terms from other, unlike, societies, but the use will conform to the basic form and rhythm and etymology of the original speech.

So what does all this have to do with writing? We write, my children, in language. We deal, what is more, with many sorts of characters, American and English, French and Russian and even non-terrestrial alien. These characters all must have language, through which they convey their thoughts, conflicts, needs, and struggles.

In order to make a western character seem to be a living person with all the traits he needs for his context, we have to make him sound like what he is. Does that mean a lot of horrendous misspellings, a' la some of Zane Grey's people?

Not at all. You can get the flavor of a regional dialect into your work without wrenching it out of plumb. "I don't intend to run up against no Indians" has just the same effect it would have if put "I don' inten' to run up agin no Injuns." Simpler to write, easier to read, and just as good an indicator of the origin and education of the character speaking.

If you want to put a Cockney into your story, study the Cockney dialect, find its linguistic rhythms and peculiarities, and then write it, without a lot of dropped E's and unnecessary H's. That is the best way, I firmly believe, to tackle dialect.

But never forget that everyone has his own tricks of speech, his own accent of locality, and his own way of turning a phrase. A repeated word or quotation, some twist of language can identify a character as firmly as a birthmark.

In order to affirm your sense of your own words, it is often useful to read your work aloud. If you can read into a recording machine, that is even better, for then you can listen critically to dialect, to sentence structure, to the flow of the narrative. And that can help you to achieve that fine edge of excellence for which we all are striving.

CHAPTER TEN

CONFLICT

To all too many editors and critics, nowadays, conflict means only one thing...physical violence between individuals or countries or systems. With this in mind, most of them recognize as a "real story" only a piece of work that incorporates into itself that sort of overt and obvious conflict.

This is a shame. There are many sorts of conflict that can be expressed in multitudes of ways. A human being in conflict with nature can find himself all too truly involved in life or death struggle. Stories involving only one character can be vitally gripping, if the other participant in the struggle is the weather or the terrain or earthquake or hurricane—or a combination of any such elements.

Stories, be they genre or non-genre, can contain the conflict of the characters with their circumstances. This can provide the most compelling and intriguing sort of fictional battle imaginable and can encompass many kinds of situations. They can also contain the conflict within a single character, and this forms the basis of a great many fine tales, both in the mainstream and in genres. Man against himself is perhaps the most intelligent sort of fictional conflict.

To create interest in a story, you do not need to thump either your character or your reader over the head with a club. You need not drop bombs or otherwise indulge in physical or verbal abuse. Conflict can also be subtle and delicate, filled with almost intangible tensions and counter-tensions.

I have seen more conflict developed at a quiet tea-party than you can possibly imagine. Three most ladylike people indulged in subliminal verbal needle-thrusts, and the battle was as definite—and bloody—as if they had been using swords. It may even have been more painful.

This, too, is conflict.

A story usually creates its own variety of conflict, as it spins itself into your mind. Overt or indirect, internal or external, it will become a part of your tale without your having to think of it in terms of a technical device. When you have woven an intricate account of delicate balances and subtle intrigues, with much care and attention to characterization, motivation, and effect, of course, you can still have an editor tell you that your story has no conflict because nobody bleeds at the end.

Mark him off your list and hope that you will find a more perceptive (or older) editor someplace down the line.

Writing an action story and writing a tale filled with the less overt kinds of conflict are not the same sort of thing.

For an example of a book containing both internal and external conflicts, both written superlatively well, you might find Ernest Haycox's *Bugles in the*

Afternoon. This is a historical novel set in the west (misconstrued and ignored as a western by many) that deals with a man who is involved, by the end of the book, in the Battle of the Little Big Horn.

It begins with a tense situation between the sergeant, who is actually an officer who was cashiered from the army, and the officer who arranged his disgrace, knowing him to be innocent. The two turn up at the same post in Dakota.

In elegant, understated prose, Haycox exposes the hackle-raising dislike between the two. For a very long while, both keep a tight rein on their feelings, and it is only after a considerable length of time, which is filled with fascinating material, that they come to blows.

By the time you reach the end of the book, the Indian battle is almost an anticlimax, for the personal control maintained by the sergeant and the interpersonal vendetta form the thrust of the tale. The resolution is not what you might expect.

In addition, his battles with Dakota blizzards can give you some idea of the REAL sorts of conflict inherent in our life on earth and dealing with nature.

When all is said and done, however, even understated or internal conflict is not actually necessary to make a good and interesting story. There are many superb stories that deal with solving problems—Man Against the Problem.

Many mysteries are of this nature. Many mainstream stories also use this as a hinge for the plot. Any kind of tale can be written so. In such a story, conflict is not the point—characterization is. Sherlock Holmes is a brilliant case in point. Many science fiction stories also used to be written around an all-engrossing problem and the character(s) who solved it. Unfortunately, too many editors and publishers in that field are now caught up in the conflict syndrome.

In the literary field, there are a great many books and short pieces that have neither conflict nor an involving problem to be solved. I cannot say that I like or can read all of this variety that I have encountered. I don't feel that fiction is best served by long, rambling accounts of dreary people trudging through drab lives or regarding their own navels ad nauseam, but a lot of those have been published. Some involve wonderfully fine writing, and yet, for me, the sense of story does not exist.

A good recipe for writing conflict is the use of your own common sense. Know your characters and what they would do in almost any given situation. Would they react with violence? Then let them. Would they chew their nails and weep? Show them doing that. Let them act out their own lives, violently or peacefully, ingeniously or brutally, as their own natures might dictate.

Conflict is many things to many people, and only you can write your own prescription for it.

CHAPTER ELEVEN

SPELLING AND ALL
THAT GOOD STUFF

In the good old days, a talented but insufficiently schooled writer could send his great novel to an editor at one of the grand old houses and know that someone up there would edit his magnum opus with loving care, eliminating grammatical errors, spelling problems, punctuation poops. Those days are far behind us, now.

First of all, the editors themselves are extremely busy people, overworked and understaffed. Secondly, many of those under forty are insecure in their own command of grammar and spelling, which also holds true for some copyeditors. Though all mean well, the press of time and lack of manpower means that fewer and fewer people shepherd a book through the publishing process.

This leaves the ball in your court. Anyone who wants to write should first polish up his/her command of written English. The Writer's Digest School conducts a basic English course that can be extremely helpful to would-be writers. This is a good way to go, if you can afford it. If you can't there are others.

Many handbooks of English are published and on the market. All are good. Perhaps the best of all may be the Strunk and White's *The Elements of Style*, which is thin, easily carried, and can be flipped through in a trice. *The Little, Brown Handbook* or *The Harbrace College Handbook* are also excellent. For a knowledge of the structure of a sentence, this sort of book can be most helpful.

There is an invaluable little book called *The Misspeller's Dictionary*. Though it has gone out of print, it is a wonderful help, if you can find it in a used book store. It starts out with every possible misspelling of almost any word you might be trying to look up. When you find the incorrect way in which you would have spelled it, it refers you to the right one. It is small, handy for desk or pocket, and there are no definitions, making space for many, many words. I recommend it highly for anyone with spelling problems.

A new convenience for the insecure speller is the *Franklin Speller*, an electronic gadget that is instant and pocket-sized. Or a spell-check for your computer word processing program can be a great help., though it will not distinguish between from (which you did not mean) and form (which you did).

I have heard writers worry that their Muse might be frightened away by too much emphasis upon the technically correct use of English. That is like a carpenter fearing that his own creativity would be stifled by the efficient use of a power saw or a nailgun. Language is our main tool of the trade, and if we master it early we will write it with far more ease and grace than do those who continue to regard it as "the enemy."

It is quite possible for editor, copyeditor, proofreader, AND YOU to go through your manuscript many times without catching potentially embarrassing errors. There is nothing more painful than finding gross errors in a published book, as all too many writers have learned the hard way. If it seems to be too much trouble to get everything right the first time, remember how you would feel with a book out there that is going to make anyone who reads it believe you to be illiterate. Then dig in and correct.

CHAPTER TWELVE

THE WORD IS THE POEM IS THE KEY

There is nothing so sadly overemphasized and simultaneously misunderstood in all of modern day literature as the symbol. Teachers of literature and creative writing, expositors, critics, all dissect the works they examine, laying out the symbols, bare and bleeding as the innards of a frog, for the instruction of students. And, with all the pontificating, none of those pinned-down guts ever show anyone how the poor thing HOPPED.

The impression is left that those who wrote the works in question deliberately and cold-bloodedly chose all those symbols before beginning the story or book or poem and incorporated them consciously into the settings. Although there possibly may be some rather anemic stylists who might do such a thing, it is by no means the way a creative artist works.

Every life is a web of symbols, most of them unique to one single person. Language itself is a symbol, standing in the place of the fact or idea it expresses. Every word in our language has private connotations for every one of us, to some extent, although the major meanings are sufficiently universal for communication.

My English language is unique to me, as yours is to you, for no two of us experience exactly the same set of emotional responses in the company of the same words.

We think in a stream of symbols, which are, in turn, made up of symbols that stand for sounds. Even if we think in pictures or in mathematical concepts, those, too, are symbols. When we write words onto paper, particularly if they encompass some inner vision about which we feel strongly, our own personal symbolism must, perforce, go onto the paper with them.

Straightforward symbolism, such as simple language or the alphabet or arithmetic, gives little trouble. The thoughts are communicated. It is when we try to reach across the gap to convey to others matters that deal with the subconscious, the infinite, or the imaginative that problems arise. That is when the intended communication can be obscured and the thought misconstrued.

A teacher digs for the symbol in order to clarify the intent of the author for the benefit of the student. That is a laudable aim. The symbol, the use of linguistic elements, the individual connotations, if they can be found, can be most useful for understanding the thing conveyed. There is no problem with attempting just that.

It is when the expositor becomes carried away with his own cleverness and begins inserting his own interior connotations and deriving from the result his own interpretations that he invents a symbolism that is not the author's. That can further obscure, instead of making clear, the matter he examines.

It is in teaching young writers that this dedicated pursuit of the symbol can be most perilous. The beginner is left with the idea that he must load his work with symbols in a purposeful—almost cynical—manner. Otherwise how can it qualify as literature?

Yet those who have written the works they are studying spoke onto the pages the words that rose into their hearts and minds spontaneously in the process of creation. True, they may later have rewritten, polished, and agonized until they brought the work into final form, but it is most unlikely that many, if any, of them ever took an early draft of his work and patched into it an intricate network of symbols.

What the beginner may not realize is the fact that his work, whatever it is, contains his own personal symbolism. He is writing in his unique language, out of the context of his own experience and conditioning. The symbols are implicit, whether or not anyone alive can interpret them correctly.

It can be a humbling experience to have the symbolic meaning of one's own work explained by one whose life is devoted to winnowing out the merest hint of a symbol. The things that you may find in my work are probably not those that I put there, on that deeper level where inherent symbols lie. Every person who reads that work is going to find a different interpretation there, if his perceptions are not clouded by some teacher who demands a cut and dried response rather than that of the heart.

Yet, below it all, the harmonics of my own life exist, seen or unseen, known or undiscovered, forever.

Perhaps the best way to deal with the question is simply to write your best and most effectively. Express your thoughts in the way that seems most comfortable to you. Then leave the symbols to academics, who will find in your work things you never dreamed were there.

CHAPTER THIRTEEN

VIEWPOINT

Nothing seems to bewilder a novice writer more than the subject of viewpoint. The process is really simple, but the concept has been swaddled in twaddle for so long that an aura of impenetrable mystery seems to surround it.

First of all, I must point out that the rules for viewpoint were not laid down by Moses when he came down from Sinai. Viewpoint as a consciously employed technique did not exist, I daresay, until the Twentieth Century.

Good writing came first, by aeons. Then the academics invented viewpoint to explain what it was that Dickens and Thackeray and Goethe were doing. So don't let it intimidate you. You may be the one to invent an entirely new and unheard-of viewpoint that will have professors pontificating for the next hundred years.

Put as simply as possible, viewpoint is the place where the writer places himself while he tells his story. That can be inside the person to whom the story is happening, thus: I never thought I'd have the chance to sky-dive, but here I stood, skin goosepimpling, heart thumping, about to step out of a plane at five thousand feet.

Or it may be in a person very close to the principal character in the story, told as events happen and he perceives each incident. This is a sort of second-hand view of the action. It is slightly more difficult to do this, for you are constantly tempted to move over inside the head of either the main character or one who knows something vital to the story. You have to remain within the boundaries of the viewpoint character's mind and his senses.

That technique goes something like this:

> I could see Joe sweating, as he waited for the signal to jump. I thought he was crazy. Never in a hundred years could anybody get me to jump out of a plane from five thousand feet up. Or even from a thousand feet up! But there he went, tumbling out of sight, and I only prayed that the parachute had opened. I was afraid to look.

You can, of course, shift viewpoints, though in a very short work this is not very effective and can be confusing.

In a book, however, it is entirely possible to have a number of viewpoint characters, each one pivotal to the plot and necessary in some way to the working out of the story. Yet no matter how many viewpoint characters there are, you need to have one dominant in each segment of the tale, and there needs to be one among them all who is of overriding importance. You are working here in what is called limited third person viewpoint, which is strictly limited to that single character's perceptions. You know his thoughts, and you feel with his senses, almost exactly as you would in first person. Every time you shift from one viewpoint to another your manuscript needs to be divided physically—a new chapter, a line of asterisks, an extra space, or italics can indicate the change.

The third major viewpoint is the omniscient viewpoint. You, as the writer, are suspended on a cloud above the action, seeing everything that goes on, knowing what is in the minds of all the characters. This used to be almost the only technique used in fiction. It now is out of fashion, some considering it dated. Used with consummate skill, however, it can still work well, at suitable times. It has been taught as holy writ in college creative writing classes that one can never change viewpoint within a single story. Many writers still blanch at the thought. But there are many stories that cannot be told in a single viewpoint, be it first or third. Yet putting these into omniscient viewpoint can dilute the impact of the story.

The input of many characters is needed to report the things they have seen and experienced. This allows a three-dimensional picture of the situation you are trying to communicate. It is in this situation that you approach the basic storyline from several angles and several characters' perspectives.

Some maintain that a first person story loses characterization for the "I" character. I disagree violently. This can give the reader an inside view of the person as nothing else can do. It also forces you as the writer to view the action from a more personal and subjective stance.

You know not only the character's strengths but his weaknesses. You feel with him his fear or his joy or his rage. Some of the finest books in English have been written in the first person.

In general, for a beginner the limited third person may be most useful, though there are stories that demand first person by their very nature. This gives you a consistent frame of reference and requires you to mind your P's and Q's when you want to jump over the hill to see what is happening over there.

Some still allow the writer's voice to intrude into the story. This is dated, though I must admit that I love to find an old novel with a "So you see, my dear children, that our heroine is about to find danger and grief" or something similar. The "Meanwhile, back at the ranch...." method is old hat and marks you as a beginner, these days.

Sliding smoothly into another person's mind and body is a learned technique. It is akin to the method actor's trick of literally going inside the person he is to portray. You have to feel the character out. Is there rheumatism in the knees? You ache with him. Bad eyesight? You begin to squint in sympathy. As you create your character, these matters will turn up, and as you remain with his viewpoint, you must remember to deal with them at appropriate moments.

The best secret I know is to lose yourself in the viewpoint character. See through his eyes, feel with his senses, react to the situation within the logical pattern you have created for him. Then write what is there to write. It usually works.

CHAPTER FOURTEEN

PLOT AND THEME

In its simplest definition, a plot is the shape taken by your story. It is the sequence of events that presents your characters, reveals their backgrounds, shows their problems, and leads the reader through all the complexities of the story to the solution of those problems.

It can be attacked chronologically, which is the simplest and best for a beginner. It can also come in nonsequential segments, welded together over the length of the tale to make a coherent whole, through the skillful use of such devices as the flashback.

If you are a real storyteller, you will usually find that your stories work themselves out in intricate detail, either beforehand as an outline or as you write. So don't worry about plots...a good one is instantly recognizable. If something that seemed promising turns out to be a dud, don't sweat it. We all waste some effort, but it is all practice that helps us to deal more effectively with our next project.

A plot can be built, just like a child's house of blocks. You introduce your main character, find his immediate interest/problem/difficulty. In a short story there may be only one, but in a novel you will need several. You may even need several minor characters, each with a problem that affects, in some way, the overall story.

Once you understand the situation with which your protagonist must deal, then you can work out, step by step, exactly the way in which he will tackle it, the obstacles that will get in his way, the other people who interfere, and the final and climactic situation in which he either conquers or accepts his own circumstances.

There is a rather mechanical way in which to add suspense and conflict. Give that character a break and make it seem that he has surmounted his problems...and then pull the rug out from under him. Create a wavelike undulation between triumph and near-tragedy (modulated to suit the sort of tale you are telling). The sequence of events can develop your character's strengths and his intelligence. It can try his emotional stability. And the protagonist and his solution can arrive together at the end of the tale.

This is useful for a beginner, but do not feel that you have to stick with this format. Some of the best stories spin themselves out in your mind, forming their own shapes and rhythms. There are incredible numbers of kinds of stories and as many ways in which they can be told. As Kipling said, "There are nine and sixty ways of constructing tribal lays, and every single one of them is right!"

Remember that you are the only person who can write your story, and once you develop your ability to professional standards nobody can tell you that this is the wrong way to do it. Not and make it stick.

Make the plot work for you, and make it fit your characters. The newspaper every morning and the news every night can be full of plot ideas. Nobody need ever go without the raw material for a story, if he keeps his eyes and ears open.

On the other hand, a theme is something frequently overlooked by the novice writer. It is integral to a mature work of fiction (or, indeed, nonfiction), as you can prove for yourself by reading some of the themeless works now sprouting on the newsstands.

Most themes can be stated in clichés. Clichés become such because they are so true and so succinct, and the underlying premise that forms the thread upon which your story is strung must partake of some bit of human truth.

Do you recall Dickens's *A Christmas Carol*? It has several themes, one of which is, "It is never too late to change." Another is, "Money alone cannot make you happy." Most stories and almost all books have more than one theme, if you look closely enough. In your own work, you may be able to look back, as you near the end of your labors, and see several interrelated themes wound through your story.

It is a strange thing that seldom if ever do you think out your theme at the beginning of your work. It develops, along with the plot and the characters, as you work. Yet, if you are deeply involved in the story you are telling, the lives of the people about whom you are writing, you will find that a theme twines itself into it, without your having to think about it consciously.

A story that is all theme would be very dull work. But a story without any at all is taffy candy for the mind. Keep a watchful eye on your work and analyze it when you are done. Make sure you dig deeply into your subject, so as to tap the thematic stream that runs beneath all good stories. Make your plot complex enough to be interesting, yet not so complex as to become soap opera.

Flashback, mentioned earlier, is a most useful device in creating a nonsequential plot. It is, however, often done very badly, at too great length, or at a point at which it interrupts the flow of the story. A long flashback at the very beginning of a tale, for instance, can make the reader forget just what was happening to the protagonist at the spot at which he went into this reverie about the past. The past must become the protagonist's temporary present, in order for a flashback to work well. For instance:

> Jonathan looked both ways, hesitated, and then set his right foot into the street. He had never quite recovered from that terrible day....

> The truck swerved into the wrong lane, heading directly for him, as he tried to spring back to the safety of the curb. Tires squealed on wet pavement, and as he squirmed desperately backward, something immensely heavy and painful crossed over his foot and ankle. The blackness that rolled over him came as a welcome relief....

> Jonathan looked down at the warped and twisted leg. He couldn't go on reliving that instant of his life forever, he knew. With a sigh, he stepped awkwardly into the crosswalk and limped to the other curb.

This is flashback. Brief ones are best, usually, but there are stories that are very long flashbacks.

Some highly effective work has been written using a sort of mosaic of plot elements, demanding mental alertness on the part of the reader. Kurt Vonnegut's *Slaughterhouse-5* is a good example of this technique.

This, however, is not something that you learn to do. It must come as an inevitable way in which to approach the story you have to tell.

Any or all of these techniques can work for you. Just have the nerve to play with them, practice with them, and make them a part of your repertoire.

CHAPTER FIFTEEN

SYMBOLISM

Having been a poet all my life—literally, since the age of two, when I would sit at the dinner table with my father and cap his lines with rhyming ones to form long sagas about buzzards and grasshoppers and crawfish—I came into the writing of fiction with an arsenal of poetic devices at my command. Whether or not you like or write poetry, those devices can make your work stronger, more compelling, and more fun to read.

Earlier, we spoke about strong nouns and verbs, unusual terms that carry their own connotations. A poet uses such words constantly, trying to make the most effective possible use of his limited space. This makes for extremely strong and intriguing work in poetry, and even more so in prose.

There are a number of figures of speech commonly used in both poetry and prose. The simile (similar comes from the same root word) is a phrase that likens one thing to another not usually associated with it. The wind was like a tiger, rampaging through the forest. The young woman was as slender and near-transparent as a fairy. The poodle was like a fluff of cotton candy trotting down the street on four stick-like legs.

While seemingly similar, a metaphor does not say that this is LIKE that. It states that this IS that.

> She was an aged monkey, scrambling about her dingy cage of a room. The world, that morning, was a dungeon, and he was the prisoner confined within it.

See how different these descriptions are from those flat-footed ones that might have been used: "The old woman was shriveled and skinny, but she moved quickly about her dirty room." That isn't all that bad, but it hasn't the effect of the other statement.

Or:

> He was terribly depressed, that morning, feeling somehow trapped in his life.

Okay, but still lacking the impact of the metaphoric sentence.

A metaphor can also be used as an adjective, when this is suitable: His granite skull prevented him from understanding.

You can exaggerate fantastically, creating a hyperbole: "I have told you ten thousand times not to slam the door!" You can make inanimate things seem animate, as in: "The wind battered at the door as if trying to come inside where it was warm." This is known as personification.

Perhaps the most useful and enjoyable device of them all is onomatopoeia, which simply means a word that imitates the sound of the thing you are writing about:

> The bucket splashed into the well.
> The wind clattered the shutter against
> the window frame. I squished through
> the wet in my leaky boots.

Every one of these matters can be used to wonderful effect in writing prose, and fiction in particular. You can make your scenes come to life in the most effective way, if you will use this sort of technique. Not in every sentence, mind you. That would get old very quickly. But often enough to keep the reader aware and awake, wondering what will come next.

CHAPTER SIXTEEN

TRANSITIONS

A transition marks a change—in place, in time, or in viewpoint. It takes your characters and your story from one point to another, and there is no need for going into much detail en route, unless something vital to the plot is involved.

Back when the motion picture industry was new, the camera followed the characters everywhere they went. Out of the house, down the steps, along the street, up the next set of steps, into the next house involved in the script.

And then came D. W. Griffith, the brilliant director, who had the idea of showing his hero going down his own steps and then immediately up his neighbor's, without the dreary trek down the street. That technique, pared close to the bone, can be used profitably by a writer.

All too many times I find beginning writers describing how George walked across the room, turned the doorknob, opened the door, and went out into the hall, where he stood indecisively, biting his nails.

Now we all know how to leave a room. Only if George must find a way to escape from a sealed chamber does there need to be any mention of how he does that. We all know that you turn a knob or something similar to open a door, and few of us walk through solid wood, so he had to open it. Why tell us about it?

So why not something more like this: "George rushed from the room, only to stand in the hall, indecisive, biting his nails." Neat, effective, and brief. That got George out into the hall, where I wanted him to be, in about half the words. If you want to remove a character from New York by train and send him to Boston, you might show a scene, if there is a necessary one, in the station from which he departs. And then you might well set him in the Boston station, trying to locate the person supposed to meet him. He might arrive at his destination by taxi, thinking about how short the trip was because he had a wonderful book to read. Any brief device can reflect the lapse of time and the movement over distance.

Changing viewpoint, on the other hand, requires some signal to warn the reader that the head he will inhabit next is not the one he has just known. You can skip a double/double space. Or you can insert three asterisks to indicate the separation of viewpoints.

In working with a novel, it is usually best to separate viewpoint characters physically by use of chapter changes, labeling each new chapter with the name of the person whose viewpoint is going to tell the story. This keeps your reader abreast of the situation, so that he doesn't have to go back to discover whose mind he is inhabiting now.

If you want to change points of view along the way, try to devise a method that will allow the reader to keep track of whose he is observing at any given moment.

Making smooth and unobtrusive transitions becomes easy with practice. You can use movie techniques in your approach to the problem, writing the equivalent of a dissolve shot, in which two adjacent scenes seem to overlap. Or you can zoom in from afar, or draw back from a close-up. See your story inside your head, as if it were on film. Then you will find that transitions, as well as a lot of other technical problems, will come clear to you and can be easily solved.

CHAPTER SEVENTEEN

NEVER THINK IT WILL BE EASY

Those who read faithfully all the books on writing and selling find, all too often, that a very grim picture emerges as to the chances of success for a novice writer. While, on one level, this can be accurate, it does not take into account solid talent and great determination.

If you have the skull of a buffalo and the hide of a rhinoceros, in addition to the skill you need, you can do it. I know, for I did it, though if I had begun my career a decade or two later it would have been far more difficult.

It should be impossible, according to accepted belief, for a farmer from East Texas to sell novels in New York, short stories to multitudes of magazines and anthologies, and poetry to literary journals and poetry magazines. Some years ago, I got a letter to that effect from an academic involved in children's literature. He liked my book, but he could not accept the fact that a Texas farmer had written it.

I did it. The writing was fun, but selling it was nothing but hard and determined WORK, coupled with persistence. How was it done? Well this is the way it happened...

In 1972, at the age of forty-two, I realized at last (I catch on very slowly, sometimes) that being a poet was not only ill-paid, it was UNpaid. Love the craft as I might, increasing postal rates were squeezing me out of the business.

My family had moved from Texas to Oregon. There was no family there; no old friends lived near enough to visit. I worked as a proofreader at the afternoon newspaper in Salem, though we lived in Silverton, thirteen miles away.

After taking up yoga exercises, I suddenly began to write science fiction, which I had loved since the age of fifteen. Working six hours a day, commuting back and forth, keeping a two-story house, making a two-acre garden and canning the produce, and helping in my husband's service station in the evenings kept me pretty busy, but Monday was my day off.

Armed with a vacuum cleaner, I would swish through my ancient farmhouse on Monday morning. And on Monday afternoon I would sit down and write one chapter of a book. In a year, I finished two novels, *How the Gods Wove in Kyrannon* and *The Seekers of Shar-Nuhn*.

I sent off the first book, after querying the publisher of my choice, and went about my business. I never heard directly from it or the editor again.

About that time, we returned to Texas to live, and it took a bit of time for things to settle down enough for me to write another book. By the time I sold the first one, which was actually the second one written, I had written five. Being compulsive is a great help, in this game.

By 1977, I was raising broiler chickens on our ten acres in Texas, writing steadily, and marketing my work. Doubleday bought the first (actually the second I wrote, the other being still in limbo) that year and another (Yes, THAT one) the next.

I still had no agent, though I had queried a number of them, one of whom turned me down because I used a box (sent me by a friend who had been an editor) that was used by another literary agency! He assumed they had turned down the book I sent him, which was not the case.

I regularly received mailings from the Scott Meredith Agency, as so many writers do. I decided to query them. The day I got a reply from them, that ex-editor friend was visiting me from New York.

She was sitting in the back seat of my car when I came out of the post office, and she read the contract included in the reply as we headed for home.

She advised me against accepting that connection and returned to New York determined to find me an agent. She did, and that agent helped me tremendously in gaining a foothold in the fantasy-science fiction field. We parted company at last because of differences in career goals, and we are still friends.

By the very nature of things, I should not have been able to get my toe in the door of publishing. But I did, and not a little of that is due to the fact that I did NOT have early and immediate success, had no massive financial windfalls, and did not achieve fame.

I kept improving my writing fanatically, as I still try to do. Early success can be the end of improvement, I have decided, after watching a few fulminating geniuses settle into mediocrity.

If a farmer/broiler-grower from East Texas can sell thirty-odd (very odd) books and dozens of short stories in the space of less than two decades, surely others who have honed their craft, polished their writing skills, and studied the markets can do it too.

But don't ever think it will be easy. You must work hard, keep at it, and never become discouraged, no matter how hard the sledding. (Later note: Now there is the electronic publishing market, as well as the print-on-demand one, but I advise careful study of any publisher in either field.)

Originally published as a column in THE HORROR SHOW, *Spring 1986, Vol. 4, Issue 2*

CHAPTER EIGHTEEN

WHAT HORRID PEOPLE!

Several years ago, I met a lady of academic persuasion who seemed most interested in the fact that I was engaged in writing both fantasy and horror. Her questions at the time led to a letter, later, in which she continued her queries along the lines of "Have you stopped beating your wife?"

"Is it not true that people who read and write horror are the sorts of fiends who beat innocent bystanders to hamburger with bicycle chains?" is a pretty good example of her style. She was quite serious, very sincere in her firm belief that recognizing the existence of horrible matters and facing them straight-on in fictional settings was the sign of major psychological disturbance.

She was not and is not alone. There is evidently a good fraction of the populace so rigidly pinned to the immediate material here and now that any sidewise peep into other realities or possibilities knocks them off their pins.

Indeed, the regular writer of this column, Joe R. Lansdale, encountered the phenomenon when his first novel, *Act of Love*, appeared some time ago. Dealing as it did with a psychotic killer of very nasty habits, it brought him to life so persuasively, with such impact and reality, that Joe found some readers tiptoeing around him cautiously. They seemed to expect him to spring upon them, knife at the ready. How could he know so well how a madman and a murderer thought, if he was not one himself? You could see that thought bouncing around in many minds.

This shows as nothing else could how little the average reader knows about the creative process. A writer has to understand those about whom he writes, whether they are sweet young things or rabid rapists. We have to get inside those heads (and some of them are most uncomfortable places to be), see through those eyes, feel with those warped perceptions.

That doesn't turn us into monsters, believe me. Most of those I know who write about horrible things are the nicest people you'll ever meet. The sort of understanding we have to acquire in our writing careers carries over into our lives. It makes us very easy to live with, usually...we don't get angry nearly as easily as other people seem to. We take out our angers and aggressions (heh! heh!) on paper.

So the neighbor across the road is hard to get along with? We have assessed his position without even realizing it, and we say to ourselves, "If I were married to his wife (had his kids, lived with a demanding father who doesn't understand that a fifty-year-old son isn't a fifteen-year-old son), I'd be a grump, too." So we don't paste him when he raises Cain about something trivial.

It makes it interesting when one is, as I am, a short, gray-haired lady of middle years. People tend to think of us in terms of "sweet" and "gentle" and "accommodating." To meet someone who has read one of your more fiendish stories is one of life's small pleasures. Those eyes that have read of terrible things under your byline now try to match up the fictional happening with the author, whose look does NOT match her work.

Few wicked pleasures are so harmless.

As others have said before me, horror writers tend to be very even-tempered and easygoing people. But what about readers of horror? Are they, as my questioner implied, people who are longing to go out and wreak havoc on the general population?

The desire to be scared out of one's socks seems to be pretty well disseminated through the human race. From Scouts sitting around a campfire, eyes wide, listening to scary stories, to those of us who dig deep into bookstore stocks, looking for newer and nastier tales to goose-pimple by, we are, by and large, a harmless breed.

Having read for years in the fields of psychology and criminology, I have concluded that pornography (the violent, perverse sort) is far more likely to produce antisocial behavior than the literate chills of horror. Vampires, werewolves, and more modern monsters haven't the readership among criminals, I suspect, that such deliberately erotic fare produces.

What is it that we who are not criminals, not monsters awaiting our chances to raven, are looking for? It's a complex question, but I think I have a few answers.

The first that comes to mind is the simplest—we are looking for a good story that doesn't retrace the same ground covered by hundreds of tales over the generations. Originality is one of the best things to be found in the field. I don't have to be reminded that there are all too many imitations and imitations of imitations to be found on the overburdened shelves nowadays. The realities of the publishing industry have seen to that.

Unfortunately, a skilled imitator can do better at selling his work than can someone who is doing genuinely original and horrific books and stories that are unlike any of those that have been "making money" in the marketplace. The fact that all the books being imitated were at one time just such un-orthodox material doesn't impinge on anyone on the buying end of the game. That is a small horror story in itself.

Yet there are works that spring up by sheer force of excellence. There are writers who persist and finally win at this strange game...they turn out to be the Charles L. Grants, the Robert McCammons, and the Karl Edward Wagners of the future. That's where our craving is satisfied.

There are other reasons, too. Less obvious ones, as things tend to be when they involve the deep needs of the subconscious.

We live, as we all know, in a context grown frightening to anyone who thinks at all deeply. Our world is threatened by politics and poisons. Our cities are wracked by crime and crookedness and mental disorders fit to make us cringe at the thought of them all.

Everything from the computer at the bank to the traffic on the way to work can throw a monkey wrench into our lives, financially or physically. Through, remember, no fault of our own. If there was ever a time when only the guilty suffered, it ended long before I began to notice the world around me.

We all know, subconsciously, that we are likely to be snuffed out in an accident, wrongfully accused by anything from the local police to the IRS, given cancer by the pollutants which we had nothing to do with putting into the air.

We live at the surface level of a complicated chain of supply that could be wrecked so easily that it makes one shudder to consider it. A relatively minor change in the overall weather patterns could send us the way of the dinosaur.

So where do we look for comfort?

Some read romances, whose cheerful endings are guaranteed, no matter how many travails are met with along the way. Some bury themselves in history, which if not more inspiring than our own time is at least over and done with. Some look outward into space and consider black holes or inward to quantum physics. There are many avenues of escape from the worries that beset us.

Horror gives one that the boldest of us can take with some advantage. It lets us face horror on its own terms, eyeball to eyeball. We are, with book in hand, in control of the confrontation. We can, if necessary, turn on all the lights or close the curtains or even, at need, close the book until we recover our composure enough to proceed.

Here is something we are doing voluntarily. No outside authority is imposing it upon us. We are approaching this abyss of terror because it is what we choose to do, and we can do it in our own ways, whatever those might be. In so doing, we are exercising those abilities that are useful in dealing with actual fears and traumas.

I don't know if such exercise actually makes a person more effective in dealing with the hard roads and tight spaces of his life, but at the very least it makes us feel as if it might. And comfort is the name of this particular game. Anything that gives some psychological balm in this excruciating context has to be a good thing. A funny side-note seems to be that when life is truly dangerous, physically...when you are immediately subject to peril to life and limb...horror hasn't seemed to be on the ascendant.

During the Second World War the most popular reading material seemed to be westerns, with mysteries and meditative mainstream novels just behind. If I recall correctly (and I was a teenager at the time, so my reading might be a bit out of the main line), there was a lot of the romantic and heroic involved in literature. It figures, if you think about it for a while.

Now our dangers are not so obvious. We suffer more in our minds than in our bodies. We are offered few opportunities for heroic behavior, and the perils we face are not dependable ones. We might get mugged in the park...and then we might not. It's more like a gamble than a war.

So we must face those tribulations on their own level, that of the mind. We need to prepare our inner selves for the onslaughts they suffer every day.

Some, like my letter-writing friend, might think this a silly way to confront our lives. That's her and their privilege. Every one of us has a different way of meeting the challenges in our lives.

Perhaps I'm a horrid person for "making up" all those terrible tales about nasty things and nastier people. If nothing else, it gets all that nasty out of my own system...and at best, it may help someone out there to get his act together to meet the worst our culture can dish out.

I can think of a lot worse things to do.

Originally published in STARLOG, *April, 1986, Issue #117*

CHAPTER NINETEEN

BUILD AN ALIEN

Most imaginative fiction in the science fiction/ fantasy genre deals, at some time or another, with creatures or intelligent beings that do not, in actuality, exist. By far the greatest number of these turn out to be derivatives of mythologically based beings—elves, winged horses, Medusae, dwarves—all the fascinating creatures that ancient myth and legend have created.

However, the most intriguing aliens are those that exist only in the writer's mind. These, once committed to paper, are entities that would never otherwise come into being. In addition to being interesting to read about, they are most wonderful to invent.

There are two basic angles from which one approaches the creation of an alien. One can first envision a planet with interesting differences from Terra, then find the attributes that would be necessary for effective survival and action on such a world.

For instance, let us assume that we have a world of constant tectonic shifting, making for earth-quakes, vulcanism, the rearing and shattering of mountain ranges, the rising and sinking of conti-nents. The air, predictably, might well be inimical for human beings, but that need not preclude the possibility of intelligent life. In fact, such stressful conditions might make life there become intelligent quickly, out of sheer self defense.

First of all, I suspect this environment would produce a life form whose body chemistry is unlike any we know. Its system might breathe—if sul-phides are what it uses in its life processes—but our alien might absorb all its needed elements through ingestion/excretion, or even take its gaseous re-quirements through its integument.

It could not have the sort of vulnerable skin that we have, and fur would be unlikely in such an at-mosphere. Chitin would be most sensible for our alien's outer layer. Chitin, with membranous vents that absorb what gases are necessary for its exis-tence, could admit the necessary portions into the system and reject the rest.

Nourishment would of necessity be provided by minerals, possibly algae and fungi as well, so this creature isn't going to be a predator. Not a carnivore (meat being unknown there, anyway), it should be a relatively peaceable creature whose intelligence might well be focused upon the survival of its off-spring.

What might it look like? Remember that chitin. Think of the ever-unstable ground it must traverse. I envision a crablike creature, probably the size of a large dog, though built very low to the ground.

It would have to be agile. Its jointed legs (probably six or eight) would need to be extensible, capable of springing great distances at a split second's notice.

Given its exoskeletal build, this alien could not be viviparous. Yet to lay eggs in any sort of place on this undependable world would be an invitation to disaster. So let us hypothesize an internal arrangement for incubating eggs.

Internal? Or maybe attached to the exterior! Suppose that the female (let's keep this a two-gender species for simplicity's sake) extrudes tiny ova from a special tube that places each one exactly in place on her shell, gluing it down with a natural substance somewhat like beeswax. These ova are placed in neat rows, over the rear half of her carapace.

For fertilization, the male might spray a liquid containing his own genetic traits over the female's back with another specialized external tube. Then she would wear her offspring as they developed to term, at which time they would split from their capsule-like containers and anchor themselves once more to the maternal parent.

She, being responsible for the next generation, would devote all her energy and her intelligence to assuring the survival of herself and her precious burden. Would the male concern himself with this? Probably not. In so dangerous an environment, that would seem impractical. Every male would probably disseminate his genes as widely as possible.

If the female proved able to keep most of her offspring alive until they reached a point at which they learned to be independent of her, what method would she use to insure their survival as adults?

This is not going to be the same thing as a cat teaching kittens to hunt. The surroundings are too hostile. Perhaps the young, as they ride high on their mother's back, observe her methods of finding food, of avoiding earthquakes and streams of lava and displaced oceans. That being true, when the time came to dismount and go about their lives, each small alien would be ready with a mind full of observed phenomena to meet its needs.

But, you might object, such beings would not really be intelligent—they could create no culture.

Culture and intelligence are not synonymous. Intelligence can be shown in many ways. Perhaps, as they wander over the constantly shifting landscape, the mother alien is transmitting to her children, through telepathy or sound or even organic transfer of information, the history of their kind: dreams and longings, possibilities and problems. The transfer of data from one organism to another in a purposeful manner is an indication of intelligence. So there you have a basic requirement satisfied.

I admit that the alien we have created in this instance is one of limited fictional use...perhaps. But given the difficult context, it is what would be necessary, and it is a good example of the stringent requirements of planetary attributes.

The other angle of attack is that of beginning with the alien and creating it to suit fictional needs. This isn't hard to do, if you happen to have that sort of mind. But once that is done, you must work backward to find what sort of world could logically have given life to this sort of creature.

That alien must be a logical product of a logical world, or he is made of purest cardboard and will not work fictionally.

One such alien cropped up in my novel *Khi to Freedom* (Ace Books, 1983). Thheeer was an energy-gas intelligence, having no body to speak of. He seemed, when enclosed in a force-field bubble and visible to human perceptions, to be a loose collection of tiny electrical sparks that flashed like minute bolts of lightning.

Because of unusual circumstances inherent in the plot, Thheeer had to make contact with a human being and gain his help in escaping from unbearably boring conditions. The difficulty, even given telepathic ability, lay in finding some common basis for communication.

A bodiless being, generated on a low gravity, desiccated, electrically charged world, has no physical needs other than avoiding moisture or too intense gravities. How can he find some way to link his thinking processes with a body-bound man, subject to fears and traumas inconceivable to one not trapped in flesh?

Thheeer cannot conceive of hunger, thirst, weariness, any form of sexual need, pain, or even anger. But he does understand boredom, for both he and his counterpart are bored out of their skulls by their present situation. That provides the necessary link and the driving need that eventually gives them communication.

Thheeer came first. That low gravity world, with its constant winds generating magnetic energies, coalescing particles of dust and eventually arriving at a sort of mind, was waiting behind my alien for discovery. The logical source of such life was there, somewhere in my subconscious, I presume, at the point at which I arrived at Thheeer. All too often, aliens are dropped into stories for effect, without the necessary thought and care. It is most unsatisfying to read about a really unusual being, see it moved across the page to serve the author's purpose, and never find out its origins, its real purposes, or its actual nature.

At this point in my writing career, I am finding myself more interested, in many cases, in my aliens than in my human beings. After all, we know all too much about our own kind. Millennia of history have proven Homo Sapiens to be a less than admirable creature in many ways.

It is not only interesting, it is absorbing when you can create your own intelligent entity, giving it some of the attributes we find lacking in our own kind. The creation of beings with very different faults, virtues, and drives is, it seems to me, a most useful thing. The exercise gives, if nothing else, a different angle of vision toward our own tendencies and our own foibles.

Originally published in FANTASY REVIEW*, September, 1984, # 71.*

CHAPTER TWENTY

TERRA INCOGNITA

In the years since I began going about to science fiction conventions, meeting people who, like myself, write of things possible and impossible, I have learned something interesting about a large fraction of my peers. They are so far removed from the realities of this world (I am not speaking sociologically) that they have no feel for it, no true notion of our status as ecological organisms.

It explains much about high-tech SF. It explains why some writers get so antsy if you propose solutions other than technological ones for the problems we face. And technology is only as effective, as "moral," if you please, as those who wield it.

The solutions arrived at are only as good as the intentions of those doing the solving. In all too many observable cases good intentions have been nullified by bad judgment.

I suspect the whole syndrome is caused by the removal of most of the population from farms to cities, over the past fifty years. So many of those I meet or with whom I correspond are totally city-bred. Everything they have dealt with for all their lives has been mechanical-technological-unnatural.

Such a context gives the illusion of control—you can sterilize a hospital ward, channel traffic, remain indoors in inclement weathers. The world of soil and weather, of animals both wild and tame, of drought and flood and tornadoes is as remote as the moon.

What all too many know of the world they live in has been learned from books. Better than knowing nothing at all, perhaps, but altogether inadequate for understanding what it means to be a living creature dependent upon a skinny envelope of air and soil and the vagaries of weather and wind for continued existence.

Sadly, when one who is a farmer to her bones, as I am, tries to communicate something of that alternate reality to those unfamiliar with it, they grow terribly uncomfortable, as if I were trying to proselyte them into some esoteric religion.

Only those of us who have spent our lives in hand to hand combat with land and weather can know without doubt that control is the most ridiculous of assumptions. We cannot control rainfall on any long-term, usable basis. We cannot prevent or turn aside the devastating track of a tornado. We cannot even get a reliable handle on the umpteen viruses that live in the soil and wreak havoc on crops and livestock. Every time "science" comes up with a cure for one disease, four more are discovered.

This is not to say that every bit of help doesn't count. It does, and will continue to. A reasonable amalgam of scientific know-how and farming "feel" does very well. We are in better shape now than in the past, though excesses are doing damage that will have to be paid for in the future.

However, no matter how many tractors, pesticides, chemical fertilizers, or inoculations are in use at any time, no farmer pretends that he is in control of his environment.

And that is where too many hard SF writers go off the track. They set up colonies on strange worlds, and in too many cases they keep their colonials huddled about a spaceport, waiting for supplies shipped in at ruinous rates. When they do attempt to set up a real, viable system, which inevitably includes a farming base for survival, they seldom do it convincingly—to a farmer, at least.

For years, stories have been postulating an Earth tamed to human purposes, weather-controlled, completely subjugated to our desires. Only one completely without experience of the world we live on could imagine—or want—such a system.

Even now, after hundreds of years of study, we don't understand what we have to work with. Every year or so another seemingly irrelevant factor falls into place as a *sine qua non* for life on Earth. Premature planners would eliminate unpleasant elements, given the chance, only to find, too late, that they were necessary, and that they have thereby eliminated us from the system, along with much else.

It might well be that the schism between fantasy and science fiction of the hard-tech kind divides along a very real line—that between those reared in close contact with our world and those from urban environments. Fantasy says, "There are things out there that nobody understands and nobody can control." High-tech says, "Any matter of interest to human beings can be manipulated and controlled by the proper use of technology." Of the two, the fantastic assessment comes nearer the mark.

The only common element the two possess is the human factor, and more and more high-tech writing is robotizing the people. Such writing gets into print, but it doesn't work well, while other high-tech stories (Bova's *Millennium* comes to mind) work wonderfully because their people are deeply human, real, three-dimensional.

The same phenomenon can be seen in fantasy—one has only to read any of the Conan pastiches, then go back and read Howard's originals. The difference between flesh and plastic is immediately recognizable.

Contrary to hard SF assumptions, this problem has no solution that I can see. Those without a feel for the physical earth cannot take some kind of transfusion to give them the necessary linkages. And we who have those linkages cannot be quite comfortable with stories set in artificial contexts, or based on false premises.

After trying to communicate with the high-tech writers of such matters, I have found that it is I who become classified as alien and strange. And so I am, but not because I know the nitty-gritty about living with the land. Something about my position seems threatening to them.

Maybe the recognition of such a dividing line may open eyes on both sides to unsuspected things. There is a deep difference between urban and rural people. Not so much, in these days, of education, nor of knowledge of the world—TV has seen to that.

It is a difference in experience and perception that goes to the roots of the individual. The lady who, interviewed on farm policy, said that she had no interest in farmers, she got all her food at Safeway, is not alone. Her numbers are growing.

I recently read a scathing attack on a government study of earthworms, by an urban politician with some influence in such matters. How many urban types realize that without the earthworm, life as we know it would be impossible?

If you are one who didn't know, you might need to get a flowerpot and plant a seed or two. Trying to grow something might give you an entirely new perspective on the things you write about and the way you attack them.

Originally published in EMPIRE, *1985, #34.*

CHAPTER TWENTY-ONE

THE WHY OF IT

Of recent years, there has grown up a kind of irritable fractiousness between those who prefer science fiction and those who prefer fantasy...as if there might only be room in the world for one of those literary genres.

Long ago, a scholar-friend made a most piercing remark that seems to have application here.

He said, "Science tells us what and how; religion tells us why."

That precise difference lies between science fiction and fantasy, which are, indeed, almost exactly analogous to science and religion. The two fields are complementary, not competitive. And one's preference is almost directly attributable to the amount of the metaphysical that there might be in one's nature.

Most science fiction deals with things physical. Technologies, wars, economics, spaceships, robots, and men who deal with such things in a dogged, determined, usually admirable but notably unheroic manner. Even as you and I deal with our bank's misprogrammed computer or the car that won't start in an emergency. Plain people dealing with extraordinary problems and equipment can usually fairly well define s-f.

Fantasy, on the contrary, and I'm speaking of the originals, not the clones of other fantasies, deals with people and the impact of their circumstances upon their characters and spirits. And, as well, the impact of their characters and spirits upon the circumstances about them.

Therein lies the major difference in the two subgenres. For fantasy deals also in the heroic – the grandly heroic, indeed. Not, necessarily, that of kings and queens and powerful sorcerers...the best presents small people faced with terrible dilemmas that force them to grow strengths and abilities that they didn't know they had.

Look at the Hobbits in Tolkien's trilogy. Look at most of Andre Norton's protagonists. There are too many more to name. Most of them deal with those who begin little and cowardly and end up rather larger and far more courageous.

Another matter divorcing the thrusts of the two matters is that of control. Science fiction presupposes that Man can eventually obtain control over his environs, whether planetary or otherwise. This, as I have stated elsewhere, is most likely an outgrowth of the urbanization of much of writerdom.

Cities can tend to give that illusion, at least insofar as dealing with "natural" forces is concerned. It is quite normal that those nurtured in cities should carry that mindset forward with them into their work.

Fantasy is, I maintain, much more naturalistic. It says, "There are things in the Cosmos that cannot be controlled. There are things out there that are immune to logic, contemptuous of mathematics, ignorant of our rituals and potencies." And that is a thing that all who live near the body of the planet know all too well.

I wonder if many of the best fantasists have not lived, at least for a time, in the country? For those who must live with drought and flood and tornado and hail and all the many things nature can fling at the farmer know that, indeed, "There are things that cannot be controlled."

I cannot say that the same problematical division exists between readers of the two. But there does, very likely, exist quite as definite a schism. It probably divides down a line in the spirit, one side of which contends that the proper activity of Man is the control of externals, the other side of which maintains that the proper activity is the control of self. And that is a heavy subject, very unpopular in today's world.

I have met those involved in the sciences who jump like tweaked cats at the mention of something like: "The solution of our ills lies, not in artificial drugs and pesticides and machinery and computers, but in our own spirits."

They seem to think that the only concern of a spirit must be religion, which is, of course, in very bad odor in the current faddism.

It is almost impossible to convince any of those that the concern of a spirit is itself. Not in a "gimme" sort of manner, but in a "how can I improve myself to the very best that I can be?" sense.

We are seeing the result of the lack of self-examination of the spirit all about us. Ineptitude runs rampant, and it gives the inept no pause or concern.

Dishonesty in business, in government, education, publishing, shoemaking, and coal mining and all points in between is so rampant as to have become the norm, not the exception.

So what chemical or mechanical miracle is science to pull out of its oversized hat to solve this dilemma? So far it hasn't acknowledged the existence of the problem.

Thus, perhaps fantasy, which is the oldest of literary disciplines, may hold the most hope for pricking a few chinks in the self-complacent wall of our culture. Not as religion—perish the thought!—but as a key to self examination: A suggestion that being normal and unimportant needn't preclude the possibility of being heroic. It can be a source of hope for something better, both within ourselves and outside, if we heave to and clean up all our acts, personal and public.

This is not to imply that s-f cannot and does not do exactly this kind of thing. It does, at times...but less and less frequently. The ability of the genre to hold up a skewed mirror to the world and say, "See how ridiculous you are?" has all but been lost or mislaid.

Its old zest for taking hold of things and making good come from ill seems to be oozing out of it. A dark vision, a sort of "What's the use? We're all lost, anyway!" seems to be taking over in all too many cases. And that which is sheer antic fun seldom carries the bite of satire, any more.

Mistake me not! There is a whole lot of sheer crap written in both fields. That has always been true and probably always will be. Sturgeon's Law has not been repealed, however much we might wish it could be.

And there are still people of moral courage and steely character walking through both kinds of stories, those who stick to their guns, no matter how rough the going gets. If you don't believe it, meet Navigator Jael in Jayge Carr's *Navigator's Sindrome* and Frodo Baggins in Tolkien's *The Lord of the Rings*. One does not have to be Odysseus to be a hero.

So it is obvious that any "conflict" between the paired sub-genres is totally spurious, manufactured, I fear, by those who want to seem to be doing the intellectual "In-Thing," or else promulgated by self interested writers who fear that their own kind of work is going to suffer in sales because of competition from the other sort. Both attitudes are beneath contempt.

To scorn fantasy is to scorn the very mythologies that are the foundation of our culture. To scorn science fiction is to scorn the myth-making of the future.

In this time of divisiveness in most human affairs, it is time to say, straight out, that a good book is a good book, be it fantasy, sf, western, suspense, mainstream, or, by God, juvenile. Let's stop bickering like a kindergarten and put our backs into writing the very best books we're capable of writing.

The time for bibs and diapers should be far behind us, and the whole universe lies before us!

Originally published in STARWIND, *1994.*

CHAPTER TWENTY-TWO

BUILD A CULTURE

It is entirely too easy to base social, religious, and economic systems needed for science fictional demands closely upon the one in which we exist. This, after all, is the world we know, the way we live, and the pattern that formed our thinking. Yet when one begins inventing alien beings and worlds, such cultural patterns sometimes are no longer suitable for our needs.

It is not easy to begin from square one and invent an alien system, even after you have created your alien species and a suitable environment for its development. If it has a culture, the one thing you can be sure of is that it will not resemble ours in any obvious way.

An excellent way in which to build an interior storehouse of potential cultures is that of studying the multitudinous societies in which our own kind lives now and has lived in the past. For this purpose, reading in the fields of anthropology, archeology, and psychology are very useful.

I have gone into my own library and picked at random some anthropological, philosophical, and other titles, which I will list here. Every one of the cultures dealt with contains matters that seem entirely alien to us in the present time in the United States of America. Some of the variations can be twisted just a bit and made to fit alien life-forms on other worlds, at need:

Sacred Mysteries Among the Mayas and Quiches, Auguste Le Plongeon, Wizard's Bookshelf, 1973

The Hellfire Club, Daniel P. Mannix, Ballantine, 1959

Ancient Mexico, Frederick Peterson, Paragon Books (Putnam) 1979

The Art of Crete and Early Greece, Greystone Press, 1962

Warrior Herdsmen, Elizabeth M. Thomas, Norton, 1981

Dead Cities and Forgotten Tribes, Gordon Cooper, Philosophical Library, 1952

History's Timeline, Crescent Books, 1981

The Iroquois Book of Rites, Horatio Hale, Univ. of Toronto Press, 1963

The Origin of Consciousness in the Breakdown of the Bicameral Mind, Julian Jaynes, Houghton, 1976

The Structures of Scientific Revolutions, Thomas S. Kuhn, Univ. of Chicago Press, 1970

The Death and Rebirth of the Seneca, Anthony Wallace, Vintage, 1972

The Forest People, Colin M. Turnbull, Doubleday Anchor Books, 1961

Man's Rise to Civilization, Peter Farb, Dutton, 1968

Archaeology: Discoveries in the 1960s, Edward Bacon, Praeger, 1971

The First Americans, C.W. Ceram, Harcourt, Brace 1971

Ancient Times: A History of the Early World, Breasted

Of course, there are many, many more, but this gives some idea of the breadth of material available to anyone interested in learning what humanity has been, what it is, and why it became as it is. As a general rule, anything by C. W. Ceram or James Henry Breasted is not only chock-full of useful information, it is also fascinatingly written.

Now you have read, let us say, a number of books about strange and unusual peoples who actually live or have lived on our own world. You want to create a logical and believable culture for a species living in another solar system—perhaps even another galaxy—and have it feel real to the reader.

This world, let us say, is fairly hospitable to life, yet it has an axial tilt that means the winters are very long and severe and the summers terribly hot and, because of great ocean basins that provide a lot of cloud cover, humid. The people who live here are reasonably humanoid, though they are covered with sleek fur, which protects them from the cold in winter and sheds to a light down in summer.

This species is semi-nomadic, fleeing the worst of winter's ravages and summer's steam baths and ranging from northeast to southwest and back across the more temperate regions of this world.

Now, here we find that they will not build elaborate cities. Their lifestyle will not need or want heavy construction that cannot move with them. They will probably use something resembling the Amerindian teepee or the Mongolian yurt, a structure easily assembled, very well designed to keep out the weather, and easily disassembled and moved from place to place.

Here let us go to the American Indian for our pattern. As it was the work of women to dress and cut hides to build their housing, and as they did all the garnering, much of the snaring of small game, and all of the farming, if any, in many tribes the women owned all the real property except for the clothing and weapons of the men. We are speaking now of pre-Columbian Indians, so there were no horses to become property.

This alien people we will design after this pattern. This automatically makes the women equal partners with their hunter/fighter men, and it precludes other than brisk inter-tribal skirmishes.

But these are not Indians. Do they have beasts of burden? Well, perhaps they have a small one, not fast enough for riding but sturdy and enduring. A very large rodent, let us say, with a most uncomfortable hopping gait, that pulls two-wheeled carts. This beast is not only useful, it can also be eaten in times of famine.

What would their social structure be like? I suspect that they have a council of elders, probably male with female advisors. Or, going back very far into our own pre-history, maybe an all-female trio that communicates with their gods.

Gods? Of course. It is only easy, civilized cultures that can afford the luxury of atheism. People living in a harsh environment need help, not to mention comfort, and that can come from some Being greater than they, invisible perhaps except in thunder and lightning and earthquakes. Ritual then becomes a part of their lives.

The cycle of their year swings from winter to summer, south to north, and let us say that every leg of their regular journey is anchored at a holy place...a small stone temple, or a pile of rocks or a megalith raised for religious purposes.

What sort of ceremonies do they hold in such a place? Prayer, of course. Chants ancient among their kind contain not only supplications to the gods but also, most likely, a lot of verbal history. Shall we make them a people who sacrifice living creatures to their gods? Life, in this context, would be very precarious and precious. No, they will, I think, sacrifice something dear to each of them. A fur robe. A metal ornament. A bright stone with swirls of mica that someone has treasured from childhood may be left on the altar—or whatever serves in its place. Let us say a circle of polished stones surrounds a pit, into which the offerings are dropped. Then, their hope renewed, the people trudge onward across a cold (or hot) landscape toward their next stop.

Would they have families that we would recognize as such? Probably not. The entire tribal grouping might be one unit, interrelated biologically. Or this might be a kind that requires three sexual partners for reproduction, and being so limited, genetically, it would probably vary those groupings regularly. So we will find no earth-style families among them.

What, then, of the young? How are they cared for and taught? Again, this being a harsh life, they will probably be nursed and educated by those too old or infirm to take part in the hard work the younger adults must do. They will, I suspect, teach the skills that will be required when the youngsters grow big enough to help with survival. As well, they will probably learn the verbal histories and genealogies with which a people without permanent physical roots pin themselves firmly into their world.

Will this be an authoritarian system that governs them? If the experiences of our own kind are any guide, it will not be. Instead, the members of the tribe will probably be independent and at least semi-autonomous. The demands of survival provide the motivation and the necessity for cooperative behavior and work. It will, if at all like the Amerindian, be a communal system, as well, caring for those who are unable to care for themselves for as long as possible.

Yet when necessity presses, harsh reality will probably prevail. The oldsters or the very ill will be left behind or will walk away on their own, allowing the food they consume to nourish those more necessary to the tribe than they.

And this, too, will say something important about this alien people on a world circling another sun. They will have fellow feeling, love of a kind, for their people. They will be a people with whom our reader can identify, to some extent. That is a vital element, in writing about alien beings. There must be some peg upon which to hang our sympathies.

We have now covered, very lightly, government, religion, education, the family, and care of the elderly. What other matters are the purview of a culture?

I suggest imagination as the most vital. Do these furred alien people look up at the stars and dream? Do they wonder what makes the gods shout with thunder and flash with lightning? If they are to be fully sympathetic with our own kind, they will need some aspect of imagination, both individually and collectively.

Let us allow them to claim a star. This is the Yellow-Fur People's Star, the lowest in the north on midsummer day. It guides them on their peregrinations. It houses their gods, perhaps. It stimulates them to great efforts in time of trouble or danger. It is their Space Program, their Party Doctrine, their dream that keeps them looking to the future.

So now we have a society, primitive, it is true, but we have had little time to work into a complex one. This same technique can be used in creating others of Byzantine complexity or Spartan discipline. An understanding of some of the many ways in which our kind has coexisted on this world over the millennia can allow us to understand those unlike us.

This is a good thing, not only literarily but sociologically. If we understand our kind, we understand ourselves and our neighbors, and to understand is to forgive, as the old saying goes.

"And why should we take the trouble to create cultures not our own?" you may ask.

Only in that way can we hold up a mirror to the things we do now, the ways in which we react to unfamiliar and unexpected situations, people unlike ourselves, without getting into philosophical squabbles with those who disagree with us. To observe a people and a culture that resemble nothing in the modern world is to observe ourselves, if things were different.

We can work out terrible problems in our own system, safely insulated from our own reality because they are happening to fictional people on another world. We can show people as they CAN be, instead of showing them as they all too often are at their worst.

That may not cure all our own cultural ills, but it cannot possibly hurt. And who knows? Someone who reads may be stimulated to do something kind instead of something stupid. That is worth the entire effort, I firmly believe.

Published in FANTASY REVIEW, *Jan. 1986, Issue #87.*

CHAPTER TWENTY-THREE

LANDMARKS ON THE ROAD TO FANTASY

To ask any fantasist to explore the question of the best work that has been done in fantasy is to invite a journey into his/her own personal past. For we are, by and large, the products of those works that set up the strongest resonances in our minds and emotions, usually at a rather early age.

For me, the road into fantasy was mapped at the age of fifteen (late, you say, and I agree, but our tiny town in East Texas didn't get a wide variety of paperback material until much later than 1945) with my discovery of A. Merritt's *The Face in the Abyss.* I can still see that book in living color, as a sort of internal movie. I know now that Merritt's style was a bit baroque for modern tastes, but anything that can evoke from a young person the reaction that book got from me has to be GOOD.

I read it a half-dozen times, back to back. I recall my feeling of triumph—"I own this! It's MINE, and I can read it as many times as I want, and the magic will still be there!"

Probably more than anything before or since (even including the immortal Alice), that book was a pivotal factor in making me the sort of writer I turned out to be.

I recall no touchstone phrases. On rereading it now, I can find basic flaws. Yet I maintain that any book that can draw from a reader such a lifelong devotion has got to contain something that partakes of the immortal. In this self-conscious age, we have tended to forget that style is really less important than story.

Of course, I immediately began looking up Merritt's work, and I did read just about all there was. Nothing had the impact of that first encounter, however. Yet he had whetted my appetite for more wonders and marvels trapped between book covers.

It was shortly afterward that I found Charles Williams. *The Place of the Lion*, I maintain, is one of the powerful, evocative, metaphysically enthralling works in book form.

From the point that I have now reached, I realize that the balance achieved between those two early discoveries set the twin poles of all my stories yet to come. Story—exciting, intriguing, involving—must be wedded to a certain intricacy of thought and perception, and the whole put into the most effective word combinations I could achieve.

Along with those discoveries came my first encounter with the work of Andre Norton. Her almost surreal worlds and aliens, her down-to-earth and understandable human characters, her swift and compelling story-lines caught my interest and have never let go. *The Beast Master* hooked me on her work. Later, her Witch World series created a fantasy context with the continuing presence and reality of a known place. Anyone who likes can mention that my work is strongly influenced by hers. I take it as a compliment.

At about that time, a burst of wonderful stuff came onto the market. T. H. White's *The Once and Future King* comes immediately to mind, with its many delights and its underlying seriousness of theme. Ray Bradbury's *The Golden Apples of the Sun*. And, of course, Tolkien's hair-raising *tour de force*.

On a darker note, I must mention the work of H. P. Lovecraft. One Christmas, about 1953 or '54, I went into, of all things, the toy department of a local hardware store. There was a shelf of books, way at the back of the place, surrounded by mechanical toys and Betsy-Wetsy dolls. They had no dust wrappers. A certain very dark book with garish purple lettering up its spine drew my hand to it...and that was the *Best Supernatural Stories of H. P. Lovecraft*.

Wow! I know, I know. His style doesn't jibe with modern taste. But he's the only horror writer to give me nightmares. His obliquely approached monstrosities, his ability to evoke a mood and to sustain it...few of us working in the field nowadays can even come near to the effects that he could achieve, much less his richly warped imagination.

Then there was *The Haunting of Hill House*, by Shirley Jackson, probably the finest haunted house story ever written. It has inhibited most of my impulses to try stories of that sort ever since I shuddered through its pages.

Then what about *Gormenghast*? Surely no one has ever invented a stranger, more fascinatingly sick group of characters and set them into a more surreal context. To have had one's father eaten by owls... how bizarre! How...interesting! Mervyn Peake's trilogy has never been imitated, as far as I know. It is inimitable...one of those original pieces of work that is so much a part of the internal workings of a single mind that it would be unthinkable to try to duplicate its effects.

At this point, perhaps I should try to reason out my own standards for fantasy. Not an easy task, indeed. Better men than I have tried and failed at producing an objective standard, so mine will be totally subjective.

For me, there are three kinds of fantasy: historically or mythologically based work that is done fictionally and becomes "real" to the reader. Evangeline Walton's wonderful retelling of the tales from the *Mabinogion* comes immediately to mind. She has made the Celtic world accessible to us as the very best history makes the ancient world come to life.

Mary Renault, in her Greek-based *The King Must Die* and *The Bull from the Sea* did the same sort of thing. One feels, reading her novels, that she must have been right there, taking notes, breathing the air, seeing with her living eyes the matters that she brings to life so convincingly on the page.

The next sort of fantasy is the here-and-now variety, of which perhaps horror fiction is most frequently found.

Stephen King is the unchallenged master of that sort of work. His *The Shining* demonstrates all the most effective traits of this kind of story.

There are others doing wonderful things with this, however. Charles L. Grant's novels do it with subtlety and style. J. N. Williamson's *Ghost* is a wonderfully moving and convincing work of that variety.

Here we come to my favorite variety of fantastic literature—the off-the-wall school of fantasy. This requires no in-depth study of anyone's mythologies. It doesn't ask that you know the here and now. It only requires an imagination that knows no bounds. Originality is often an outstanding aspect, and daring is an integral part of its workings. We live in the best time for finding that sort of work, I believe. Though William Morris and E. R. Eddison went through the roof in such works as *The Well at the World's End* and *The Worm Ouroboros*, they were ahead of their times.

Now we have such gems as Ursula K. Le Guin's *A Wizard of Earthsea* and its companions. Joy Chant has shown us *Red Moon and Black Mountain*. Peter S. Beagle has introduced us to *The Last Unicorn*. Elizabeth Moon has recounted *The Deed of Paksenarrion*.

All these contain powerful and original contexts that exist only in the writers' minds. And that, my friends, is the magic of the thing. We can visit Europe or Asia or Africa. We may even visit the Moon, one day. We can read in mythology and archeology and anthropology. But only if writers entrust their own secret worlds to paper will we ever have the chance to visit those.

This is the Golden Age of the fantasy lover. Though I knew that, all along, I kept discovering it from time to time. Several years ago, again in an unlikely spot, I found a rack of books. In a gun shop, in fact. My perceptive and well trained hand (witchery is involved, I do not doubt) moved toward a crowded shelf and pulled out a very slender book by a writer I had not, at that time, heard of. Patricia A. McKillip was the writer, and *The Forgotten Beasts of Eld* was the book.

Once again, in mid-life, I experienced that mind-blowing feeling of discovery, of excitement, of triumphant EUREKA! For this is a book so cool, so cleanly written, so crystalline in concept and execution that it fills a fellow writer with envy. I wish I had written that! is the accolade, and I gave it at once on reading the book.

Every time I find myself thinking that all the avenues of fantasy have been explored, all its intricacies mapped, I find once more that I am wrong. In the past decade, there have appeared books capable of blowing away the cobwebs from minds, altering one's personal maps of the cosmos, changing one's perspectives on humanity and living and dying.

One of the best of these is Michael Moorcock's *The War Hound and the World's Pain*. Exploring the basic natures of good and evil, as it does, it ends up by making you re-examine all the preconceptions you imbibed with your mother's milk. It is not for the lazy minded.

Very lately, indeed, has come R. A. MacAvoy's *The Book of Kells*. For sheer inventiveness, using a Celtic context slightly askew from those with which we are familiar, it is fun. It has seriousness of purpose. It involves the reader and carries him along with its flow. A pure delight, which is one of the most important of fantasy's tasks.

So...what has all this proven about fantasy...or about my perception of it? Perhaps the most important demand I make upon the field is that it says something about people. Something perceptive or fantastic or true or possible.

I want it to say something worth hearing. If I want to reread Tolkien, I will go back to the originals. I don't want clones. If I want it to make pointed comments upon the human condition, I can find many writers who will satisfy that craving, and for that I don't have to go to fantasy.

From fantasy I want more. I want human truth robed in wonder and crowned with strangeness. I want contexts unlike those everyday ones we can see all around us. The very alienness of imaginary surroundings brings to life the humanity of those in the stories I love.

We all struggle, day to day, with mundane problems. We need more intriguing things upon which to set our gazes. The achievement of maturity. The discipline of self. The ability to be kind and yet firm with those we love. The capacity to reject self-interest in the pursuit of justice and virtue.

Those are worthy goals that are beaten to death in ordinary fiction. It is in addressing such matters that books like Lillian Stewart Carl's *Sabazel* and Joan Slonczewski's *The Door Into Ocean* succeed. Their alien intricacies bring new life to old concepts.

For fantasy is, when unwrapped and held up to the light, simply allegory in a new guise. And we who have read and been shaped by the best of it have, I hope, absorbed, along with the wonder and the strangeness, a sense of fitness that has been all but lost in much of the mundane literature we see today.

So ends my backward journey through a maze of books. Many have been omitted for lack of space. Many authors have not been mentioned, for no one knows the entirety of the things that influence him. I will wake tonight in purest agony, asking myself, "Why didn't I mention...?"

To do the subject justice, I should mention every book I have ever read, and that would take an encyclopedia-length bit of work. For every book has had something in it that made me, just for an instant, think that this might well be the best thing of its kind I have known. I don't finish those that don't get that sort of response from my critical faculties.

Originally published in EMPIRE MAGAZINE, *Summer, 1983, Issue # 31.*

CHAPTER TWENTY-FOUR

OTHER WRITERS' DREAMS

Though many of us live part-time in worlds and contexts invented by writers who catch our loving fancy, not too many are called upon to go into those semi-alien landscapes and continue stories begun by others. Some, of course, do it for sheer love, as in the many *Star Trek* stories and the probings into Marion Zimmer Bradley's Darkover. I did it because I was asked to do it. For money. By the editor at Ace.

I must admit that I had read H. Beam Piper's work for many years and was at ease within his world and with his people. Yet I now believe that I could have done the job, even if I had been unfamiliar with the given context.

No matter how well you think you've read the original material, you find that you missed much of it in reading for fun. You must read your originals with total attention, making notes like mad and immersing yourself in the atmosphere.

In my own case, the world at hand was Zarathustra, and the people were, in the main,

Piper's two-foot-tall, golden-furred Fuzzies. It soon became apparent that Piper and his successor, William Tuning, had set up a number of characteristics for their small aliens that were never explained in any of the first three books. These were not matters that might be attributed to the nature of the Fuzzies, or at least not entirely.

For instance, they spoke in ultrasonics. Yet they COULD speak within the range audible to human ears. Why had they chosen the higher frequencies?

Being an old woodsman and animal-observer, I found the answer rather easily. On Zarathustra, I decided, predators could not hear such high-pitched sounds. Here they can, but there they cannot.

In addition, it had been emphasized that the little people were sexually promiscuous. Now this was part and parcel of the "sweet, childlike, cutesy-pooh" image that was created for the Fuzzies, yet I knew that creatures capable of surviving for over a millennium upon an inimical world filled with predators that thought them delicious had to have a lot of moxie. They had to be terribly intelligent, inventive, courageous, and just plain gritty. So there must be a better reason than "this is fun" for their sexual behavior.

According to Tuning, they were survivors of a spaceship wreck that had taken place some twelve hundred years before. So there had been just the complement of the ship as a gene-pool. In addition, there had been a catastrophic earthquake some three hundred years later that had taken another large chunk of their survivors. So there you had, at most, a couple of hundred individuals left to carry on the race. The widest possible dissemination of genetic traits was obviously advisable.

Thus it was inevitable that the "government" (though that is entirely too structured a term) of the Gashta had taken a hand, assigning breeding patterns to individuals as long as they stayed in the valley where the crash had taken place. And when the various families went out into the rest of the continent, they took with them the knowledge that this was a thing necessary to their well-being as a race.

Another thing that kept cropping up was the habit of the Gashta, when groups met in the forest, of sitting in a circle and "yeeking" at one another. This naturally had to be a matter of keeping some sense of their racial identity, individual hero-stories, songs, and remembered history in their separated state.

From the tales and songs preserved so came the material that *Little Fuzzy* compiled into the chronicle that became *Golden Dream: A Fuzzy Odyssey*. When employees of the Chartered Zarathustra Company attempted to drive a group of Gashta insane, they found it impossible to do so. Now that is a tall order. What set of circumstances might cause a bright, fun-loving, inventive, yet shallow-seeming species to become immune to madness?

I could think of only one thing, outside of hereditary mental stability of an impossibly high order. That was a policy of elimination of the unfit until that trait disappeared from the race entirely.

This, in light of our own dearly held beliefs, seems tough cookies, indeed. Shades of Hitler! And yet...and yet...given a tiny nucleus of survivors in a highly dangerous environment, it would be almost a necessity. And they HAD survived.

So we have the tale of Big Voice and his disastrously bad leadership, creating the precedent for such a policy. I must add here my own belief that the Gashta were unusually stable and that such necessary executions must have been very rare indeed.

It was the opinion of my editor, with which I agreed wholeheartedly, that the Gashta had been made to appear entirely too trivial a people. Their behavior, in those first three books, seemed lacking in dignity and self-respect. Their game-playing, their ready acceptance of the gifts, the ways, the lifestyle of their human hosts needed justification other than a simple shallowness of character. When the picture of those centuries of hardship, danger, and deprivation came clear to my inner eye, I realized that once you understood the background of the Gashta, you would understand all those matters at once.

After peril there was safety. After hunger there was food that really satisfied. After loneliness and predation, there were big, warm, loving humans to cling to, to love, and to humor.

Humor? Oh, yes. They weren't quite sure for a bit that the Hagga were not actually a super-clever animal. Once they knew for certain, they felt very sorry for our species, which had been as lonely and deprived, in its way, as the Gashta.

There were, of course, many other matters that I had to address and to explain. Never once did I find myself at a loss for logical reasons, once I donned a Fuzzy-fur. To walk in another's moccasins is to understand his reasoning and his ways of life.

There, of course, is the crux of the entire matter of walking into the dream of another and carrying it on. One must identify with it. Look about it from the inside. Find out what is under every bush and behind every tree trunk. You must smell the air, taste the waters, hear the beasts snapping twigs behind you and the birds of prey shrieking through the sky.

It is highly convenient to have a computer-type head, as I do. Lacking that, voluminous notes, which you must digest until they are a part of you, are quite necessary. Reading and re-reading and re-re-reading the original material (until it seems that you must have written it yourself) is another vital necessity.

I believe totally in the Gashta. Somewhere, in another dimension, those golden-furred, emerald-eyed people carry on their lives. I have been a part of them for a short but important part of my life. Though they came into being inside the mind of another person—or two—they have become, also, my own offspring.

And that may be the last and most important part of carrying on the dream of another. It must become so real to you that you can, at any moment, transport yourself into that milieu. This comes as a matter of course in writing your own original material, but it is a bit more difficult when fitting yourself into that of another mind.

I don't know what history Piper had in mind for his Fuzzies. I have no way of knowing if Tuning intended going into more detail of his Gashta discoveries shown in the third book. But once I was set on the track of the Gashta, they came alive for me, telling me their stories, showing me their triumphs and tragedies in full color and three dimensions.

And that makes the fun of writing, whether it be your dream or that of another.

CHAPTER TWENTY-FIVE

YOU JUST DON'T LOOK LIKE AN AUTHOR!

We can't all look like Ernest Hemingway or Dame Edith Sitwell. That's probably a good thing, too, as there are so many writers selling enough material to qualify as "authors" that it would make for terrible confusion.

I look respectable. That is, of course, most deceptive, but there it is, and I cannot do a thing about it. I am a short (five-foot, two-inch), gray-haired, grandmotherly looking old lady who should, if looks were accurate, have nothing more pressing on her mind than a batch of cookies in the oven or a patchwork quilt in progress. The result, when the truth comes out, can be funny.

Several years ago, I had a young friend who was a senior at the high school in a very small town that is somewhat past the back of beyond. No writer had ever gone there to speak to students. My friend invited me to come, after consulting with his teachers, and I spent two days there, in the fall and again in the spring term, talking to juniors and seniors in English classes.

They had been told, of course, that a science fiction writer was coming to speak to them. They had visualized, I realized later, Mr. Spock, complete with pointy ears. When the door opened and in walked an old lady who looked like their own grandmothers, I could almost hear a gentle rain of teeth falling to the floor. I was not, in any way, what they expected.

So when I had been properly introduced, I knew I had to crack that wall of expectation that here was a sweet little old person who wrote sweet little things. I read them a story that began: "My mother was eaten by wolves." That got them, of course, and we all had a wonderful time all day, both times I was there.

I, too, live near a tiny community (Pop. 300), which is not used to having science fiction writers among its denizens. The postmaster for many years was a wonderful lady who ran the best post office in the country (always excepting the one postmastered by my son Robert).

I am terminally busy, and when I get into 'town' at all, it is to run into the bank or the post office or the grocery store and out again, so few know me. I darted into the post office one morning, loaded with manuscripts, as usual, and found a new minister talking with my friend the postmaster.

She is very proud of my progress, having been my most effective "finger-crosser" through the years, and she said, "Oh, Mr. --! You must meet our local author. This is Mrs. Mayhar."

He smiled warmly and shook my hand. "And what do you write?" he asked. "Religious articles?"

With my usual lack of forethought, I blurted, "No, I write science fiction."

I thought for a moment he was going to bolt for the door.

I have a writer friend who actually had a newly introduced person run, wordlessly, from the room without so much as a how d'ye do. She, too, looks respectable.

A science fiction convention or a writer's conference can be most interesting. Authors you have wanted to meet may be there, but unless they are labeled in large letters on their badges (if you wear bifocals, as I do) you probably will never spot them.

The raciest romances are written by the most ladylike of people. The wildest science fiction and fantasy are written by people whom you would not suspect of even reading anything more imaginative than the stock market reports.

Nevertheless, it is very nice to be able to talk with those whose work you admire. They are people, never forget it, and people devoted to a very solitary craft. They like to hear from those who read and respond to their work.

That is what conferences and conventions are for, really. And if, as happened to me recently, you find someone who was misled by a mislabeled photo in a program book into thinking I was a young woman with long brown hair and learned almost too late who I really was, it can lead to very interesting conversation.

I know writers large and writers small. Bearded ones hobnob with clean-shaven ones. Lovely women writers, young and old, tall and short, wander about among fans and others who follow their craft, being regarded as ornamental adjuncts to a convention instead of integral parts of the publishing business. We are as hard to identify as editors, believe me.

But no matter how we look we share a love for and devotion to our craft. That, any way you look at us, is the important thing about us.

CHAPTER TWENTY-SIX

ATMOSPHERE, IMAGERY, AND FIGURES OF SPEECH

The evocation of a time, a place, a mood, an atmosphere can often be the element that makes a book or a story work to its best advantage for both the writer and the reader. What would Daphne du Maurier's *Rebecca* be without that overpowering sense of foreboding, of mist and fear and madness permeating that novel? What would Georgette Heyer's Regency England be without her sure instinct for recreating the images, the speech patterns, and the mindset of that era through terms suitable to its time.

Perhaps the most effective tool for creating such effects is the figure of speech. While not often mentioned with much emphasis in writing courses or books on writing, this tool, which is the backbone of poetry, is equally useful to the writer of prose. The principal figures of speech follow, together with examples:

SIMILE—the common root with the word SIMILAR gives the definition of this term nicely. Similes say that this is like that. "She was like a kitten, purring and cozy but with sharp claws concealed in her neat little paws." Or: "The night was like a black curtain, shining with cold rain and streaked with rips where the lightning tore it apart."

METAPHOR—this says that one thing IS another, totally dissimilar, thing. "She was a kitten, purring and cozy, her sharp claws concealed in velvet paws." "The night was a curtain, shining with rain, ripped with streaks of silver lightning." This can also be used as an unusual sort of adjectival device, in which a noun forms the adjective for a dissimilar noun: The pewter cloud spat rain and intermittent sleet. Across the beaten-copper desert, the sun set amid a tangle of crimson clouds.

METANOMY—this uses a universally understood proper name to denote characteristics of an individual. "'I'd better go before King Kong catches me,' said the timid little man, with a glance at his large and overbearing wife." "'The Bank called today,' she said, taking out her checkbook and frowning at the noted balance."

PERSONIFICATION is something we use constantly without realizing it. This makes an inanimate object or force behave as if it were alive: "The tornado dipped lazily and stuck its dark toe into Mr. Johnson's hay barn, which whirled away amid dust and loose hay." Or: "The automobile veered out of line and headed straight for me, its bumper sneering at me as it took aim at my cringing body."

ONOMATOPOEIA—this device imitates the sounds of things through the use of specific words. "The bait plunked into the water, and the small waves lapped against the bank."

Many words are directly derived from the thing they describe: swish, thump, flap, flutter, lisp, whisper, growl, purr, clank, grumble, rumble, rip, zip, clatter, and hundreds more echo phenomena they represent.

The use of such unusual elements gives life and originality to your work, but used to excess they can clutter your style. A restrained approach is best, dropping in such phrases at important points at which sensory elements are needed to make the scene or the background come to life. An example:

> Marilyn clung to the porch railing, feeling the greasy damp of the wood slip between her cramped fingers. Like a shipwrecked sailor clinging to a lifeline, she held on, praying that no one would come out of the house and look up to find her, an unlikely ornament, hanging against the vine-laced lattice. If someone did come and see her—she shuddered, her teeth clacking in the chill—the Godfather would soon know of it, and she might as well loose her grip now and die a clean death.

This is, of course, a mood of suspense and fear, complicated by chill and danger. But other moods can be evoked just as easily:

> Ellen bounced along the path like a red and white striped ball, her small bare feet displacing shells and pebbles as she made her way to the wavelets where her mother let her play. Behind came the Elephant, her nanny, with a

large basket of lunch for her small charge and the flock of instant acquaintances that she inevitably gathered about her on the beach.

Frequent repetition of any element becomes monotonous, of course. A mixture of several, as in the first example, makes for liveliness without repetitiveness. One or two, as with the second example, creates color and action.

Mood and atmosphere can, of course, be created without the use of such figures of speech. A judicious use of nouns and verbs, together with carefully selected adjectives, can do just what you want. Here is an example of this:

> The Baroness posed at the top of the curving steps, the dark lace of her gown accenting her slender shape, which belied her seventy years. The antique ivory of her hands moved outward as she greeted her host with, "Eh, Paolo, *che bello!*"
>
> About her, the marble columns and the sweep of steps became a stage, which she commanded with practiced ease.
>
> Below, the guests already assembled in the loggia looked up at the spotlighted pair and almost applauded, so dramatic was the gesture with which Paolo Benedetti took the arm of the venerable actress and led her down in triumph to join the others, amid a cloud

of black lace, which fanned along the pale marble, framing them in its misty embrace.

Equally useful are charged nouns and verbs when dealing with a mood of action and suspense:

> Derek dropped the last six feet, to land with a crunch in the soft soil of a flowerbed. The low voices of the watchmen cursed and muttered beyond the high stone wall, while before him the asylum slept in fitful moonlight. The first dangerous step was behind him. He edged along the wall, out of the moonlight, and once in the shadow of the privet hedges lining the walk he moved onto the paved path he found there. In the shadows he felt safe, and he went more quickly. The silent hands that grabbed him from behind almost stilled his heart with astonishment and terror.

Nouns and verbs can do wonderful things. Common ones like walked and ran, sat and said, are the mainstays of ordinary writing, and we use them constantly. But there are magical ones that can instantly create mood and atmosphere. Instead of walked we can use other verbs, each of which evokes a different picture.

> He trudged home in the evening, his head bowed with weariness.

The child pranced at the end of her leash, held out of traffic only by the desperate grip of her mother on its other end.

She crept from the room, shaken with sobs, and fled to her study.

The small boy slipped through the woods, his slingshot at the ready.

She waddled confidently forward, her skirts held in one pudgy hand, her basket in the other, waiting for the fishmonger to produce for her the best of his catch.

Nouns can contain a thumbnail sketch of the character, if you find just the right one.

The hag grinned, her wrinkles gleaming in the early light.

I caught a glimpse of the behemoth as he skulked behind a pillar.

The mansion loomed over the hut as if to emphasize the difference in their status.

"I was attacked by a Berserker!" she shrieked. "He took my purse and almost caught me in the alley."

The warrior bent over the fallen
shepherd, a hint of regret in his eyes.

Each of these not only mentions a person or a thing,
it also brings into focus a host of connotations inherent in the noun used, thus creating the individual
atmosphere of each.

A thesaurus is filled with scintillating words just
waiting to be discovered and used to make your
prose sparkle. The best writers are those who com-
bine all these elements, particularly in the leads to
their stories, in order to grab the reader at once with
both mental and sensory appeals.

Alistair MacLean's *The Golden Gate* begins by
using crisp, sometimes bi-syllabic sentences that
create his mood through rhythm, rather than imagery:

The operation had to be executed
with a surgically military precision,
marked with a meticulousness that
matched, in degree if not in scope, the
Allied landing in wartime Europe. It
was. The preparations had to be made
in total stealth and secrecy. They were.
A split-second coordination had to be
achieved, over and over again, until
they played their parts perfectly and
automatically. They were so trained.
Every eventuality, every possible de-
parture from the planned campaign had
to be catered for. It was. And their con-
fidence in their ability to carry out their

plan, irrespective of reversals and departures from the norm, had to be total.
It was.

The compulsive drive of this lead paragraph sets the mood for the book that follows it, grabbing the reader into the context and making him take part in what comes next. The alternation of long, complex sentences with those bullet-like two-word ones is highly effective for the purpose achieved here.

George R. R. Martin's *Dying of the Light* presents a visual effect and a dark mood just as effective but entirely different, in its use of poetic imagery. It begins thus:

> Beyond the window, water slapped against the pilings of the wooden sidewalk along the canal. Dirk t'Larien looked up and saw a low black barge drift slowly past in the moonlight. A solitary figure stood at the stern, leaning on a thin dark pole. Everything was etched quite clearly, for Braque's moon was riding overhead, big as a fist and very bright.

Fritz Leiber begins his wonderful fantasy, *Ill Met in Lankhmar*, with a combination of consonance, unusual hyphenated adjectives, and exotic names:

> Silent as specters, the tall and the fat thief edged past the dead, noose-strangled watch-leopard, out the thick,

lock-picked door of Jengao the Gem Merchant, and strolled east on Cash Street through the thin black night-smog of Lankhmar, City of Sevenscore Thousand Smokes.

Mary Stewart's *The Hollow Hills* begins with a joyful mood and a highly evocative situation that sets up the context for the story she is about to tell:

> There was a lark singing somewhere high above. Light fell dazzling against my closed eyelids, and with it the song, like a distant dance of water. I opened my eyes. Above me marched the sky, with its invisible singer lost somewhere in the light and floating blue of a spring day. Everywhere was a sweet, nutty smell which made me think of gold, and candle flames, and young lovers. Something, smelling not so sweet, stirred beside me, and a rough young voice said: "Sir?"

If you are not smiling after that, yours is a very dark mood, indeed.

Anya Seton's *The Hearth and the Eagle* begins with a storm, and she sets the mood deftly:

> On the night of the great storm, the taproom at the Hearth and Eagle was deserted. Earlier that evening men had wandered in for beers or rum flip—shore men, all of them now, too old to

go out with the fishing fleet. They had drunk uneasily, the pewter mugs shaking in their vein-corded hands, while they listened to the rising wind. Even more boisterous gusts puffed down the big chimney scattering fine ash over the scrubbed boards. In the Great Harbor two hundred yards away, the mounting breakers roared up the shingle, muffling the clink of mugs on the table and the men's sparse comments.

The tension here, as men wait out the violence of the storm, comes through with brevity and impact, and the noise of the storm is a character in the scene.

Kathleen Snow's *Night Walking*, a mystery, has an equally evocative beginning:

Wednesday, June 16, 1976, 11:59 P.M.

The car eased off Long Island's Highway 27, homing in on the sound of surf. The tires drilled upon asphalt, turned right, crackled onto a hard-sand roadbed. Hollies, then the mittens and gloves of sassafras flogged the car's sides. It burrowed deeper. The roadbed became a path, engulfed by masses of catbrier and twisted lianas of grape and poison ivy.

Without a single obvious word of warning, Snow has created a sense of tension and dread. The word flogged has a dire connotation. The car burrows deeper (personification) and is entangled with poison ivy, a bad omen, indeed.

As you can see from the above examples, the ways in which you employ your images, your nouns and verbs and adjectives, create your effect. A wide-ranging vocabulary. a sense of rhythm and the flow of language, and a picture inside your own mind that you become able to convey to the mind of your reader, those are the basic elements needed for this sort of masterful writing.

It wouldn't kill you to read some poetry—good old stuff like Matthew Arnold's "Dover Beach" that creates its own reality as it sings to you. Language can be used with the accuracy and skill of a scalpel, as the best poetry uses it, and second-best words never do the job you want them to accomplish.

The fact that you write prose should never limit your determination to write with the greatest possible impact and effect. A reader of fiction can be delighted with singular images and compelling moods, and short-changing him in that department cheats both reader and writer.

CHAPTER TWENTY-SEVEN

CREATING THE PAST

There are, these days, numbers of novels being published that are set either in prehistory (American or European) or in ancient or medieval history. The demands upon the writer created by those lost contexts are considerable, and I have discovered or invented a number of techniques for use when doing this sort of work.

I will begin with prehistory, for it is at once the easiest and the hardest to recreate. There are several elements that are of great importance, here. First is the terrain upon which the novel is to be set. When working, as I do, in Amerindian prehistory, this can be discovered by traveling through the actual countryside involved. The lay of the land changes, of course, but those changes come very slowly. Even if an ancient sea is now a desert, the contour of surrounding terrain is probably not too different now.

But terrain is not the only important element. When you retreat into the past, you will find the weather was far different a millennium ago, in most parts of the world. There are records of meteorological research into tree-rings, as well as scars and other marks on the land itself, that can help you discover something about existing conditions in the time-frame you want to explore. Weather, to primitives, is of utmost importance, and you need to get that as nearly correct as possible.

I use a video camera as I travel, making comments about the book in progress as I go: "This is where they would have crossed the river. This great stone peak may have been higher then, but it was right here. There in that canyon is a great place for an ambush." This helps me to keep in mind the progression of the plot, setting it into exact locations. I also make notes, both in a notebook and, when stopped at night, using a notebook computer.

This helps to keep the freshness of immediate observation:

> "The lion-colored mountains lay along the horizon, paws stretched out into the sagebrush, heads lowered to watch us as we crept past" is one such notation.

It is such reactions that give life and verve to the descriptions you will write later.

In addition, you are going to be working with people who no longer exist. Their descendants may be found among the members of living Indian tribes, or of Asian or European peoples, but you cannot push historical habits, beliefs, and rites backward and come out with anything acceptable as their primordial roots.

Human beings evolve in many ways, and present-day beliefs and customs cannot give clues to what our ancestors did four hundred or a thousand or two thousand years in the past. Europe and Asia have written records that fill in those gaps, but in most cases the Native Americans have only oral tradition, to which white people have only recently paid heed.

My method for creating those elements is this: I investigate the country itself. I look at any artifacts available, pry into museums, read anthropological and archeological works, and learn as much as I can about the contemporary weather, physical surroundings, tools, etc., used by the people about whom I write.

Then I set into that context human beings with minds at least as inventive and ambitious as our own, as well as needs and emotions that are fully human, in our own terms. The problems they face are those that would be natural at that time and place. Being real people (at least to me), they face and resolve them in logical and satisfying ways, according to their individual characters.

To understand how primitive people think, as well as the structures of different primitive societies, and in order to invent rites that are believable for them, I read a lot of anthropology dealing with tribes that have been discovered in isolated areas in the fairly recent past. New Guinea, South America, the Pacific islands, parts of Africa, and early America, as chronicled by explorers and missionaries, have all been the sites of such discoveries. The kind of behavior found among them contains certain common elements, and those are the things that can make your own primitive people, of whatever kind, feel real and natural to your readers. The anthropologist can be your best friend. The diarist or missionary or invader who kept records can be even more valuable.

To try moving back from the Navaho of today to their Athabascan ancestors is as useless as trying to learn the lifestyle of an Anglican priest of the time of King Henry VIII by studying an Episcopal minister of our own era. Principles, rather than specifics, are the things we need to search for, when it comes to human customs and behavior.

Jean Auel has given us all a solid example to follow with her believable portrayals of extremely ancient people and their activities. Her success is based upon personal research into matters of survival as well as in-depth reading, and the reality of her own experience shows through.

NOTE: One cannot always depend upon even the most prestigious sources. In *The Native Americans* (Smithsonian Books) the author states positively that the ancient peoples of the plains, from the Folsom and Clovis point-using eras, lived in specific ways, had specific customs, and required specific behaviors of their people. Since the only evidence we have to prove they were ever there at all are spear points and discolored post-sites for their pit-house lodges, that is misleading in the extreme. They were there and they were human and they made beautiful spear points—that is all we know for sure. Because of such misinformation, cross referencing is always a good idea.

Ancient history is a productive area for the novelist, as Mika Waltari found decades ago with *The Egyptian*, *The Etruscan*, etc. If this is a field in which you want to work, there are wonderful (deductible) trips you can make to see the countries and even some of the ancient cities themselves. If you cannot afford such travel, Time-Life has published a fascinating set of books called *Time-Frame* which covers periods from 3000 BC to 200 AD. Pictures of the terrain, art, inscriptions, and information about Sumer, Babylon, the Norse peoples, etc., are available through such books, which will supplement scholarly works with visual detail.

For my particular purposes, Time-Life may be the most valuable resource, for this company has published several sets of books dealing with ancient and historical Indians and their cultures.

Facts-on-File provides an *Atlas of the Greek World*, by Levi, that locates historical sites and gives information about them. Equinox has published a *Cultural Atlas of the World* series, of which I have so far found *Ancient Egypt* and *The Roman World* (both available from Time-Life).

As we work with early historical times, it is sometimes good to know what was happening elsewhere on earth during the period involved. I have two excellent books that cover a long period of time. Smithsonian's *Timelines of the Ancient World* allows you to trace, across the span of the globe, historical data from the beginning of human existence up to 1500 AD, using modern archeological discoveries to make informed speculations as to the earliest eras.

History's Timeline, from Crescent Books, traces man's history up to 1980. In order to learn what was going on in the world in 1850, the time of my newest novel, I ran my finger down the listings for the period 1848-51. This gave me the 1848 revolution in Austria, which was only one of many going on in

Europe at that time. And that gave me my character, Kristina Holzer, refugee from that revolution, in which her professor husband had been involved. Her sons in America, of course, had gone west with the California gold rush, by the time she arrived in Charleston (1849). History, as well as geography, can create story, if you know how to use it effectively.

When dealing with fairly recent history (a thousand years or less) there are translations of classic works, journals of scholars, and, when we near our own era, letters and diaries that can provide living texture for the lives of those involved.

Research is fascinating. If you write about past eras, choose those in which you are most interested, for your own enthusiasm will add dimension to your work. The secret of using research wisely is not to try putting in everything you learn. That bogs your storyline down in reams of material that doesn't propel plot or help to form characters. Snippets of detail put into relevant spots can bring a story to life as nothing else can. A bushel of data will choke down your reader and send him screaming to less generous authors.

Your aim must be to make people who are sometimes not even footnotes to history come to life in living color, so vividly that modern readers can empathize with them. Trying to put in too much data distracts from the characters and their story. Putting in too little makes your story lack depth and reality. Walking the thin line between bringing to life a lost past and overwhelming your reader with material may be difficult, but it can be done if you immerse yourself in the time, the people, and the story you are creating.

Create real people, set them against valid backgrounds, and let them work out their lives before your eyes. That is the way to make the past come to life.

Sources for Research Materials:

Mail order sources:

Edward R. Hamilton, Falls Village, CT 06031-5000 (catalog) contains books of historical and archeological/anthropological materials, as well as arts, fiction, self-help, etc. (*Atlas of the Greek World*, by Levi).

Barnes and Noble (catalog) 126 Fifth Ave., N.Y., NY 10011 contains a wealth of historical and archeological material. (*History's Timeline*, by Franklin; *The Costume Timeline: 5000 Years of Fashion History*, MANY more).

Time-Life Books, 1450 Parham Rd., Richmond, VA 23280: (sets of books such as *The American Indians*; *The Old West*; *Time Frame*; *Lost Civilizations*; *Cultural Atlas of the World*).) (No longer active)

Smithsonian Books, The Smithsonian Institution, Washington, DC (*The First Americans*, *Timelines of the Ancient World*, etc.).

The Video Catalog, PO Box 64267, St. Paul, MN 55164-0428 contains such sets as Kenneth Clark's *Civilization* series, *The Civil War* series, *Great Cities of the Ancient World: The Story of Rome and Pompeii*, etc.

NOTE: Visitors' Centers and Ranger Stations at national and state parks and monuments usually have excellent books concerning their specific areas, as well as related materials. Chaco Canyon, NM, Capulin Mountain National Monument, NM, and Ash Hollow Visitor Center, Nebraska, have been particularly rich in materials I needed.

Magazines:

Archeology Magazine, The Smithsonian, National Geographic Magazine, etc. can be found in used book shops.

Other Resources:

In order to get the incidentals correct, I buy such books as *Edible Native Plants of the Rocky Mountains*, by Harrington; *Western Forests*, by Whitney; *Mountain State Mammals*, by Russo; *Medicinal Plants of the Mountain West*, the Museum of New Mexico Press, all obtained at Visitor Center bookstores. When you visit an area, usually some of the plants, animals, trees, etc., are strange to you. Getting these right is important.

CHAPTER TWENTY-EIGHT

HOW NOT TO STARVE AS A WRITER

Almost every writer who has attained professional status has at some time had an enthusiastic beginner approach him, starry-eyed, to say something like this:

"I have just sold a story to –! They are paying me three hundred dollars! I'm going to quit my job and write for a living!"

My first instinct, always, is to grab the youngster by his collar and shout, "Don't!" with all my might.

To those who have not yet experienced the illogical ups and downs, not to mention the irregular and undependable nature, of payment for material that has been bought and delivered, it seems that once you have sold professionally, it will become easy to sell more. That, sadly, is not necessarily true.

There are several reasons. First, of course, is the fact that there are limited commercial markets for short fiction, these days. Though many magazines do publish fiction, most pay modestly for the privilege. For every market like *Omni*, which paid fabulous rates (and no longer exists), there are a hundred less remunerative publications.

In the science fiction-fantasy field, which I know best, standard rates vary from four to perhaps seven cents a word. At this rate, even a novella will bring only a relatively small sum.

Below markets paying that scale are the semi-professional and "little" magazines. Their standards, usually, are high, but their capitalization is limited, which forces their rates to remain low. A half cent to a penny a word is usually their offer. While this can buy postage, it isn't going far toward making a living, believe me. The best thing these markets can do for a beginner is to showcase his work and put his name before those who may later recognize it.

If you write mystery, horror, and science fiction/fantasy stories, there are fewer than two dozen profitable market for you to approach. There are many lesser ones, of course, that may bring in the grocery money (if you eat lightly) so that may bring the sum total of possible markets for stories in the above categories to about thirty or forty. Those markets are flooded with submissions, and the competition for space is fierce. But if you could sell a story to each of them five or six times a year, you might make a very modest living.

It doesn't usually work that way. To make a living from short fiction is almost impossible, and those who work mainly in that field often teach writing classes or something similar in order to live and work. The competition for those spaces may allow you to sell only a couple of stories a year to one of the really viable markets, if you are extremely good and fairly well known in the field.

So you dissuade that young writer from trying to make it selling short stories. "I will write books, instead. That will give me a better income, once I have sold a couple and have established my name," he will say.

Unfortunately, even after you have sold well over twenty, as I have [this was written a long time ago!], you still will not have the sort of dependable income that our economy demands of those who intend to survive without going to the woods and becoming hermits.

You cannot, for instance, count on drawing any royalties on a novel, no matter what genre is involved. Many books never make more than enough to pay back your advance (and some don't even do that well). Some companies, who shall remain nameless, write more creatively in their bookkeeping than their authors do in their novels. And if you should earn royalties, they will only be paid twice a year, in almost all cases.

This means that you are going to have to write enough books in any given year (at mid-list rates for advances) to sustain your personal economy. If your usual advance is from three to five thousand dollars, which was for a long time fairly average, you are going to have to write at least five novels a year in order to live at all. And when you are forced to work that quickly and steadily, writing becomes a chore instead of a joy.

Even if you are able to crank out that many books in twelve months, however, that doesn't mean that you will have a steady and dependable income. You're going to get great lumps of money at unpredictable intervals, with long droughts between them.

It is almost impossible to explain to a bank, a utility company, or a finance company that you are not paid weekly. Not monthly. Not even quarterly.

"I may have ten thousand dollars by June," you might say to your banker in February. "But it may take until August to get my money."

Bankers do not understand that. If you need a loan to sustain you while you wait for the advance to come through, you are not going to get it. You may have to take a temporary job pumping gas or cleaning houses in order to eat in the interval.

And that is the best reason I know to hold onto any job that pays the bills, no matter if it does cut into your writing time. Nothing, believe me, discourages the Muse like starvation.

When I wrote my first two novels, I lived in Oregon, worked as a proofreader for an afternoon newspaper, commuted seventeen miles (one way) to work. I made a two-acre garden and canned the produce, besides helping my husband in his service station in the evenings.

When, you may ask, did I find the time to write? I had every Monday off. After zooming through my house with the vacuum cleaner like a demented bee, in the mornings, I sat down every Monday afternoon and completed ONE CHAPTER of the book in hand.

I thought about that book while driving, waiting at stop-lights, between rushes on the job, waiting in doctors' offices. By the time I had the physical time to sit down at my (manual portable) typewriter, I had organized the material so well that what hit the paper was actually a second draft. I had gone over everything, not only waking but in my dreams, and the story had built up such a head of steam that it erupted onto paper.

Anyone can organize his life so as to leave some time for writing. Nobody can do it for you, of course, for only you understand your schedule and any possible holes it might contain. But you can manage it, if you devote effort to doing it, and you can find time to write, if it is only an hour a week.

When you have done that and are writing (as well as eating) regularly, you also have to begin marketing on a steady basis. If your output is of professional quality, you will begin, sooner or later, to sell. One Indication of the approach of that era will be the arrival of personal letters of rejection...even "sorry" scribbled onto a form rejection is a sign that SOMEBODY LIKED what you sent to them. Editors are busy. If one takes the time to do that, he/she liked the work and may well recall your name when you present him with another story. Which, if you are wise, you will do pretty promptly.

Sales will become fairly frequent, as you go along, and you may earn larger amounts. With novels this is particularly true, for most first novels draw very small advances, which can grow modestly with each additional book. There are few of us who have blockbuster best-sellers, and we must content ourselves with persistent, unspectacular growth in income.

The income from your job is going to be more than welcome, particularly if you have a family. This is going to remove the stress of worry about meeting bills, emergencies, and other demands, and that will relieve your mind, letting it relax into its creative mode.

One who quits a steady job to write full time, unless he has outside income, may find himself worrying full time and writing less than he would have done by working it into his job schedule.

Unless you are independently wealthy or married to a professional with a solid yearly income...or like to chew your fingernails and tear your hair... KEEP THAT JOB!

When you begin grossing six figures a year, that is the time to quit.

Originally published in THRUST, *1990.*

CHAPTER TWENTY-NINE

FROM METAPHYSICS TO MARS

There are too many readers (and writers) who seem to feel that physical phenomena are all that are important in the creation of science fiction. Those tend to discount fantasy entirely, as taffy candy for the mind, simply because fantasy deals with non-physical matters.

Yet the best science fiction deals with many things other than the physical. And fantasy ante-dates sf by millennia, containing within its long bib-liography a record of the workings of the human imagination. Both genres are valuable tools for teaching both facts and principles, as well as for opening the minds of readers to possibilities they had not dreamed of.

It is shocking to many when it is pointed out that nothing we know except the natural world would exist without imagination. To create a skin covering to keep off the wet, some prehistoric mind suddenly blinked into action and imagined such a drastic and original step.

To create an electric light, a human mind had to imagine that such a thing could be done. To send probes to Mars, the concept had to appear first in the human imagination. Modern Fundamentalists to the contrary, imagination is a positive, not a negative, force in the lives of our kind.

For one who intends to use his own imagination for writing science fiction in any of its incarnations (including fantasy), there is a best possible progression through which to pursue that goal. Scientific knowledge is a part of that, but it is by no means enough by itself. A writer of imaginative stories has to break free of the paradigms we know, of the limitations of perception that are a part of our culture.

Let us begin with science itself. It is not an entity. It is not a holy religion ministered by scientist-priests. It is a method of investigating the phenomena that surround us, both on our world and as inhabitants of the Universe.

The first scientists were metaphysicians, starting from scratch. They knew very little about the composition of matter, the movements of the bodies in the heavens, the motive powers that kept everything working.

But they thought about what they saw. They observed people and things intently, and they created hypotheses that seemed to explain the things about which they wondered. The scientific method not yet having been invented, their guesses were wide-ranging and included many things that are no longer respectable for scientists to investigate.

But they laid the groundwork for everything that has developed since, step by slow step, over several thousand years. The alchemist fathered chemistry. The astrologer tracked planets, discovered stars, mapped heavenly movements, and his work became the basis of astronomy.

Philosophy formed the foundation of every theoretical system from sociology to psychology, and those who developed mathematics from its most basic and necessary roots laid the groundwork for quantum physics. The present stands squarely on the shoulders of the past, although our historically illiterate generation seems ignorant of this.

It helps for the writer to understand that. There are many intellectual fads and prejudices in our society, not the least of which exist among those whose initial interest should be the pursuit of truth, whatever that may turn out to be. If a writer subscribes, unthinkingly and unknowingly, to those canned opinions, he limits drastically his potential for doing original and unusual work.

If we are to get to Mars, as writers, we have to understand at least the concepts of metaphysics. Otherwise we will write shallow stuff that has no underlying basis of historical reality or psychological truth.

Whether or not we ever use metaphysics, in the classical sense, in our work, the knowledge of the questioning nature of Man, the intricately interlaced systems that form our Cosmos, the open-endedness of investigation should form a part of our personal stance as we go about creating stories about other worlds "out there" or inner worlds of mysticism and magic.

We must create a kind of reality, whether it is based on scientific findings or on the needs in our species that created religion and magic. Our systems, within our stories, have to be logical in their own contexts.

An understanding of human psychology is as necessary for this as is an understanding of planetary mechanics or any other physical phenomenon. Too much science fiction, these days, is slick physics or engineering expertise forming the basis of a TV-quality plot, walked through by cardboard characters.

In contrast, a book like Ben Bova's *Millennium*, which is lived by real people who have their roots in the culture of our world as it is and has been, is an experience, not a "good read." A fantasy novel like Lillian Stewart Carl's recent *Wings of Power* contains not only finely crafted prose and real people as its characters, it also draws on an understanding of the cultural roots and philosophies of the "alternate" Indian subcontinent on which it takes place.

The element adding both depth and strength to both books is that comprehension of human psychology, philosophy, and history, the metaphysics of the books making them work to their highest potential.

So what of Mars?

Although the actual discoveries by probes on the surface of the Red Planet show a far different sort of world from that he imagined, Ray Bradbury's Mars will remain, I suspect, the Mars many readers will retain in their minds. He used his deep understanding of the ways of our world to create a delicate balance of history and character, of dream and intuition that made a world so real that it created its own actuality.

When one of us sits down to create a world that never was, we must compete with the Master. And to do that requires much more than a knowledge of the physical aspects of the thing. The spectrum of light, the kind of sun, the gravitational pull, the presence or absence of moons, the balance of elements forming its soil, the mineral content of its oceans are important, it is true, but those are things that are the merest background to the story we must tell.

Going into intricate detail about the physical aspects of a nonexistent world is not only fantasy, it is dull fantasy. It will be the people who walk there, the ways in which they deal with the situations they face, the reality of their personalities in action and interaction that will determine whether or not we have succeeded in our attempt. They must be rounded human beings, rooted, as we all are, in the world we know and carrying a cargo of preconceptions, prejudices, talents, attitudes, and conflicts with them to this new world.

Psychology is a term for one aspect of metaphysics. Studying it in a textbook is a very poor and second-hand way of learning about people. Poetry is better, beginning with Sappho and ending in the present. History is better yet, if you can find contemporary diaries and letters, untouched by the heavy hands of academics.

But best of all is listening and watching. In stores, in buses, in professional offices and planes and washaterias. The metaphysics of a redneck chauvinist are best understood by listening to him describe his treatment of his uppity wife to a sympathetic companion as he waits for his (one-person)

wash to cycle. The metaphysics of an epicene dilet-
tante are best understood by remaining sober at a
cocktail party and listening to his/her conversations
with others of that ilk.

Such knowledge can be gathered easily, if we
keep our ears open and our memories sharp. Our
treasury of character elements, each with its own
historical/metaphysical background, can be counted
over as we wait for red lights or buses or fly from
Houston to Baltimore.

For it is not the physics of science fiction that
makes the genre gain in strength as the years go by.
It is the metaphysics underlying the best of the
books and stories that give the field, one slow step
at a time, more and more credibility in the main
stream of literature.

CHAPTER THIRTY

UGLIFICATION AND DERISION

It has always puzzled me that books and stories that are based on the lowest denominator of human behavior seem to get both editorial and critical acceptance that is by no means justified by literary merit, while cheerful books that explore the saner side of humanity quite often are dismissed as unrealistic. That says something very uncomfortable about our culture and about those who shape the attitudes of the publishing business.

It isn't that cruel and evil-tempered people do not exist—heaven knows, I have encountered my share of them in the almost eight decades I have spent on this planet. But I have met multiples of that number who are solid citizens, doing their work decently and taking care not to trouble their fellows. Lowlifes are not the only creatures taking up space in the world, believe me, and why should literature, which traditionally has held up the more admirable and interesting of our kind for examination, pretend that the only reality is ugliness?

Since when has abject misery been the only human condition? Reading criticism, one would think that nothing else had a grain of truth in it, while the reverse is more nearly true. Misery is a matter that some of our kind tend to tailor to fit their own needs, and laying guilt-trips on those who can afford the luxury of a book and time in which to read it is not going to improve either those people or their unhappy situations.

The cult of "relevance" seems to be dying away, to some extent, and good riddance. Pessimism has never improved the lot of Mankind, nor has it tried to. "Such is life," sighs the pessimist, giving up without a struggle. Optimism, on the other hand, has constantly looked past the problems of the present to see wonderful possibilities lying in wait for the future.

Even when examining those involved in the seamier side of human affairs, the writer can show a balanced view of humanity. Dickens's people lived, the most interesting of them, in less than ideal conditions, and yet they are generally a jolly lot, coping with their troubles and yet keeping their tempers and their senses of humor unimpaired.

Sam Weller is the most cheerful of men, even though keeping track of Pickwick and his feckless crew must have been a Herculean labor, taxing even his lower-class good humor.

Which brings up humor. Too much has been written about the plight of the poor and the downtrodden by those who have never experienced either poverty or the condition of being stomped flat. From a comfortable study in a well-to-do home, life in a slum or a war-ravaged countryside or a southern shanty evidently seems unbearable. It never occurs to most of those writing from such a remove that humor is the last resort of the human spirit, when everything else is grim and hopeless.

Read some contemporary accounts of the Blitz in London. The people crowded into the subways and other shelters had their altercations, it is true, but they also sang and cracked jokes and, after the war, seemed to miss that forced intimacy with their neighbors.

Listen, some time when you are in a recovery room, coming out of surgery, to the interns talking while they think you are still entirely, instead of mostly, out of it. The jokes they tell are marvels of dirty wit. Mortician jokes are still worse, but they, too, relieve the tension and the stress of involvement in the most painful moments of human life. Humor seems to be the saving grace of humanity, instead of irrelevant frivolity, as too many of the ultra-serious seem to feel.

If we are to write about people as they are, let us be honest witnesses. We all know that there are good and bad people and all shades between. We know that no one person is entirely virtuous or entirely wicked, but an interesting mixture of both, one side dominant sometimes, the other at other times. Every one of us has the potential for being either a saint or a murderer, and only our own circumstances and learned control can determine which road we will follow most regularly.

So why is so much of modern fiction filled with witless wonders who do their thinking below the belt instead of above the collar bone? Why are idiots blundering into obvious pitfalls so often the norm instead of the comic relief?

I know from personal observation that most people enjoy knowing (and reading about) fascinating people doing interesting and constructive things. Why else should novels like Elizabeth Forsyth Hailey's *A Woman of Independent Means* have been such a success? It contains no scandal, no ugly and self-seeking motives, none of the salacious (and boring) material that encrusts all too much of the work we see today.

Selfish and short-sighted characters do not live interesting stories. It is as simple as that. Look at prostitutes, who have woven their way into public perception as the only really interesting female characters (a matter that may probably be laid to the last gasp of male chauvinism).

I know a few. They make their livings below the belt simply because there is nothing above the collar-bone with which to survive. Dull is too kind a word for the ones I know. So here is fiction creating an impression that is very seldom true.

Of course, I can see people behaving in unbecoming ways, every time I look out onto the street. Why on earth should I invest ten or twenty (or even more) dollars in order to read about more of the same? Who needs that?

I much prefer to read about tough people doing their best, giving life their best shot, win or lose. Yet if I write such a story and send it to an editor, chances are that I will never sell it. Admirable people, winners or losers, are not what the fiction market wants. Even normal failings, such as all of us display, seem inadequate to make editors feel that such characters are "real." Such failings are respectable ones.

What is wanted, I have come to believe, is someone "just like everyone else," for which I read "just like all the worst impulses of everyone else." Such a character can evidently make both editor and reader feel that his own nasty habits are less repulsive (or no more so) than those of the protagonist who shows all the worst traits he can muster while dealing with his life and problems.

That has never been my perception of the purpose of literature, no matter what the genre. While I want reading to be fun, I also want it to be demanding and never totally comfortable. It should make us look at ourselves critically, challenging us to improve our circumstances. And it should give us something important to think about when we are alone.

Not that every book can do that—and not that every book that intends to accomplish that can succeed. But a story that tries to accomplish that much is admirable, whether or not it succeeds. On the other hand, a book that is intended to make villains feel comfortable because they read about worse villains is not one that I find acceptable or useful.

There is a perception among some that a book intended for pleasure reading is absolved from the obligation to say something valid about people. Those who decry science fiction (and they are many, though their numbers are dwindling) do not understand that it is possible to say something really pointed about some of humanity's worst failings, when you give those traits to an alien species and then deal with them constructively. You can slip the mickey to your reader without his ever becoming aware consciously that you have told him something nasty about himself. Yet you hope that, subliminally, something of what you say will stick inside him.

Today we decry the hypocrisy of the Victorians. They maintained a guise of ultra-respectability, and yet their private lives were shocking to a degree that is almost incredible. Nowadays, it is *passé* to speak of good and evil in direct terms, of right and wrong behavior. Our watchword is "do your own thing," which can lead, in time, to utter boredom. Without the knowledge of sinning, where is the fun in licentiousness? And if sin should prove to be no fun at all, then why not try virtue, for a change?

The Victorians had those concepts well defined. Everyone knew exactly what constituted proper behavior and what was not. Large numbers of them indulged in the most improper behavior with augmented gusto, simply because it was sinful and thus more fun. They chose to sin and they did it and never looked back.

In our world, all too many of us don't even know what ought to be sinful behavior. And if writers cannot give them yardsticks by which to measure themselves, their behavior, and their circumstances, who is going to? The schools do not. The churches have lost any credibility they ever had. Technology solves mechanical, not human, problems. Only literature is left to reflect us as we truly are and can be and perhaps should be. Only in books can we find that desirable state that some can find sometimes and others almost never.

If the pictures we hold up to reveal our culture to itself are done in nothing but shades of gray, we will be doing an extremely poor job, and the dollar-sign values of publishing will bear a heavy burden of the guilt. This is a world full of wonder and pain and beauty and terror, and it is our task to bring it to life as it appears to us in this age and at this time. Such works endure and show our distant descendants how we lived and who we were.

I doubt that most of the books being published now will last (even if the paper upon which they are printed might) for fifty years, much less for centuries. And, considering the content of so many of them, it is probably desirable that they be forgotten as quickly as possible.

Reality changes. People change. Time wreaks irrevocable alterations. A good book can tie one era to the next, with affection and understanding, but a bad book is best left unwritten.

CHAPTER THIRTY-ONE

GENRE GYMNASTICS

Each field of fiction has its own style, voice, and tone. To give some indication of genre differences, let's set up a situation and write scenes: western, science fiction, mystery, and horror.

A young woman, fleeing an abusive marriage, must find work to support her son. She would like to live in the country, for Jonathan has allergies, and she thinks he would be healthier in a cleaner environment. A legal secretary before her marriage, she sends out resumes in reply to ads from small towns. She receives several replies but chooses to interview with a young lawyer who has expressed interest. The scene will show her first encounter with James Lowestoft:

Western (changed to make it fit the era):

Julia reached for her portmanteau and turned to her son. Jonathan wheezed as he came down the steps from the train, for the air was thick with smoke and cinders. There was also a strong smell of manure from a horse hitched beside the platform. [This sets the era.]

The boy was constantly ill in Chicago. She knew he needed clean air, but this was certainly not that! She wrinkled her nose and saw a skinny young man in a crumpled suit and string tie hurrying toward her.

"Miss..." he glanced down, saw Jonathan and amended that to "Mrs. Harrow?"

He looked more like a farmer than the Judge in Chicago, but she held out her hand. "I am Julia Harrow. This is Jonathan. Mr. Lowestoft?"

He gave her gloved fingers a nervous shake and retreated as if she might bite. "Yes, ma'am. I brought my buggy. This all your luggage?" He gestured toward the cases on the platform. When she nodded, he dropped them into the back of the vehicle.

As they rolled, amid clouds of dust and any number of flies, toward the dingy hotel, Julia found it in her to regret her hastiness in coming. Judge Raines, her former employer, vouched for him, but surely Jonathan would find no culture in such a backward place. Yet she must find work, and few lawyers were willing to hire a woman, however experienced, as secretary-clerk. [This establishes attitudes toward women at this time.]

The boy suddenly began wheezing. She took him across her lap and pounded his back. Lowestoft looked down, concerned. "I didn't really understand about the boy," he said. "When I read your letter I was so desperate for somebody that it didn't occur to me to think about him. But this is a healthy place, and I'm on the edge of town so the dust isn't so bad. The boarding house is next door. If you stay, you can arrange with Mrs. Warren to live there until you find a house."

That was a kind thought, and she reconsidered her first impression. There was intelligence in those pale eyes. A considerate employer would be a blessing, after those long years of abuse from Herbert.

There came a frantic bawling in the distance; a cloud of dust boiled up ahead of the buggy. Lowestoft pulled into an alley as three animals went pounding past, driven by a dusty yahoo twirling a rope and yelling as if the devil were behind him. [This establishes the locale and atmosphere.]

Yes, she thought as she wiped the grit from Jonathan's pale face, they were in the Wild West. She wondered if she, bred gently in Boston, mistreated in Chicago, tossed here like flotsam, would be able to cope with this as she had everything else.

This is NOT going to be a romance. There will be no romantic attachment with the young lawyer. The plot may concern her coming to grips with the different customs of this place or with her struggle to keep her sickly son alive. Her husband may even reappear on the scene. Gritty is the key word here.

Science Fiction:

Juli felt her stomach rocking slowly back to equilibrium as she sank down the lift-shaft from the shuttle. Her son gripped her hand desperately as they looked about at this new world, on which they must learn to live, if Jonathan were to survive at all. The reduced pollen count, the light gravity, the advanced medical treatments available here would surely help the boy overcome his allergies and strengthen his weakened heart. [That makes it obvious that this is science fiction set in a colony on another world.]

She surveyed the crowd of people waiting for those disembarking from the shuttle. Where was her new employer?

Lowestoft—a strange name, harking back to old Terra; these days few remembered that fabled planet. A tall shape pushed through those waiting for clearance. He was thin, rather scruffy looking, as if he didn't give much thought to his appearance. That had to be her new boss, the one lawyer in the known systems who looked poor. He stopped when he came within hailing distance and asked, "Mrs. Harrow?"

Juli nodded. "You are Attorney Lowestoft, I'm sure. This is my son Jonathan."

Jon wheezed and began to cough. Instantly, the medic from the shuttle was there, setting a mask over his face and pumping in oxygen to relieve his spasm.

"We'll get you through clearance as quickly as we can," Lowestoft said. "My wife has ordered a meal; then your living space should be ready. It seems the boy needs rest."

He grinned shyly at Jon, and Juli thought that this was very unlike the lawyers for whom she had worked during her short, unhappy marriage. He looked kind and a bit absent-minded. Was this move, desperate though it had seemed when she undertook it, going to work for them at last? She thought about that as she worked her way up the line, received her handful of inoculant pills, and accepted her luggage, which had been inspected and stamped as free of contaminants.

Lowestoft was waiting in a hover-car, as the attendants heaved the cases into the carrier. Jonathan, impressed,

clambered aboard. Already, his breathing seemed easier.

This changes details to suit them to the time and
place. The tone is quite different from the western
scene, and the attitudes of the characters have been
adjusted to conform to this advanced era. The plot
will involve unusual and perhaps alien characters
and situations.

Mystery/Suspense:

She checked the platform before
stepping off the train. Behind her Jonathan whispered, "Is he there?" What a
horrible way for a son to feel about his
father! But that was behind them, she
hoped, as she took her case from the
porter and helped the boy down the
steps. This was a clean new beginning.
The old abuses and terrors were back in
the city. She had covered their trail,
and even Herbert wouldn't be able to
trace them.

She pushed Jon toward the station,
keeping among the departing straggle
of passengers. The habit of caution was
so ingrained that Julia wondered if she
would ever be able to relax and behave
like a normal person again.

A thin man came down the platform, his gaze flicking from face to
face. Not Herbert. She relaxed slightly.
"Mr. Lowestoft?" she called.

He turned, and his keen eyes took them in with one quick glance. "Mrs. Harrow! You look tired. May I offer you tea before we have our interview? The boy looks pale. I suspect he needs something solid inside him."

She felt a surge of gratitude. Jon coughed, holding his mouth with both hands, and she handed him one of the drops his doctor had prescribed. "That would be very nice, Sir. We've had...a long trip."

But even as she followed the barrister toward his waiting automobile, she felt the pressure of Herbert's unseen pursuit. He would not stop searching. How long could they hide from him?

Here there is tension mixed with danger, from the first line. The contemporary time period is obvious without being stressed, and the situation in which Julia finds herself comes clear very quickly. The mystery will probably involve Herbert. Will he find them, and if so, what will he do?

Horror:

The office was in a building so old the brick was crumbling; mortar fell like rain on the walk before the front door. The entry hall was dark; Julia knew she couldn't leave her son there while she interviewed for the job. No, he must go up those forbidding stairs with her. Perhaps there would be a place for him to wait.

The door to the elevator was of wrought iron, and the cage beyond looked so flimsy and unreliable that she refused the thought of taking it. The two of them began to ascend the creaking stair, whose treads were worn through to the wood. Julia cursed herself for trying to find work in a small town. However ill her son might be in the city, it had to be better than this morgue of a building, with its smell of ancient polish and Lysol.

The upper hall was cleaner, with windows at either end. Though the linoleum tile on the floor was worn, it had been scrubbed inexpertly, and the door she faced was newly painted. A young lawyer, just beginning his practice, had to rent what he could afford. She felt sudden sympathy.

Julia tapped on the door and entered. The outer office was well lit, and the desk waited, bare and hopefully dusted. Again she empathized with the youngster now trying his wings. Surely, with her experience, she could help him. She tapped at the inner door, which snapped open so suddenly that she flinched.

A narrow face, framed in flyaway blond hair, peered out through thick spectacles. "Mrs. Harrow?" The voice was thin, almost a squeak.

"Yes. Do you mind if my son waits here? He was a bit nervous downstairs."

"Of course, of course. And you may come in here with me. There may be magazines..."—he gazed absentmindedly about the outer office—"Do come in."

Seating herself in the chair beside the scarred desk, Julia examined this odd young man with interest. He had the air of an academic, but there was sharpness in his gaze that belied that.

Their interview was quick; he offered what was, in her present circumstances, a living wage. She could provide him with her long experience with the Judge, who had now retired. Before she could change her mind Julia accepted the position.

Jonathan need not come here ever again, if it made him uneasy. She could surely bear a moldy old building if it would get her son out of the city, which seemed to devastate him.

She smiled and held out her hand. "Then it's a deal, Mr. Lowestoft. I hope we can make a go of this. The Judge began by using his dining room for an office and writing his briefs on the table; they had to clear it before they could eat."

The narrow face creased into a grin. Then Lowestoft sobered. "Mrs. Harrow, there's just one thing. This place...it isn't terribly safe." [The first eerie indication.]

She nodded. "I wouldn't risk the elevator," she agreed.

"And the stairs aren't too secure, either."

"It isn't only that." He bent forward as if to emphasize his words. "There are other things. Mrs. Harrow, don't ever go down into the basement!" [This is the grabber.]

"But why should I want to? And if I did, what danger could there be?"

He shook his head, his hair fluttering wildly. "I can't say more than that. But remember, I've warned you."

Here it is easy to see the elements beginning the tension that makes horror work. The moldy old building, the elevator that strikes a chill into Julia's heart, the disappearance of the child all make for mood and atmosphere. Those two elements, more than anything, create horror.

You have seen a number of variations on a theme, each aimed at satisfying the needs of a specific genre, though there are many approaches to each. Matching style and details to the story you want to write will increase its impact.

But wide reading in the desired field is necessary and researching the specifics of era and genre is vital. Those are what allow you to achieve the effect you want, making your voice speak in the manner most suitable for your tale.

CHAPTER THIRTY-TWO

WHAT'S IN A NAME?

If you are a devoted reader and find that you are not finding books by your favorite mid-list authors on the shelves, there is a reason. If you are one of those mid-list authors and your agent tells you that the publisher wants your next book to appear under a pen name, there is a reason. If you are an unpublished writer, you may find yourself in an unexpectedly strong position for marketing your first novel, and there is a reason for that, as well.

The business of writing and publishing has changed dramatically in the past decade. Old-line family owned companies have been acquired by multinational corporations, whose concern is the "bottom line," rather than the quality of the fiction and nonfiction their acquisitions will produce. As many of those corporations are owned outside the U.S. (Bertelsmann in Germany comes immediately to mind), this means their concerns are removed from considerations of readers' tastes and stylistic standards.

In addition, the big book chains have revolutionized bookselling in this country. Aside from WaldenBooks, B. Dalton, and Crown, there are sev-

eral smaller chains (Hastings, BookStop, and Publishers' Warehouse, for instance) whose buying
policies now control, to a fairly great extent, the
purchases of manuscripts made by the publishing
companies.

The purchasing systems used by the buyers for
these chains, who are few in number and buy for all
their outlets in this country, impact us as writers
more than anyone would have thought, a few years
ago. The computer, bless it as we may when doing
rewrites, has turned out to be the snake in the grass
in this particular area.

The buyer, finding a new book listed on a publisher's release, punches up the author's name, last
title, and number of copies shipped of that last book.
The number shipped for the prior novel determines
the number ordered for this new book, no matter if it
is in a different genre or if the publisher has promo-
tional plans for it.

A middle of the list title last year can ruin the
chances of a big breakout sale for a lead title this
year. The buyers will not place enough copies to
support sales efforts on the part of the company.
Under an author's own name (or regular pseudo-
nym), that breakout book will not achieve your goal.

Because of this, your agent will approach you,
asking for a pen name. An unknown name stands a
better chance at getting wide distribution than does
a well known but non-best-selling byline. For that
unfamiliar listing, the buyer will have to look at the
publisher's placement of the title on its list and its
plans for pushing the book. In theory, a lead title
position will cause him/her to order enough books
to go around.

This system has a lot of in-built flaws, which the publishing and bookselling industries surely must realize, in time. By losing that familiar byline, both businesses lose the audience that follows that author's work. School libraries tend to stick with authors whose books are suitable for their needs, yet without the recognizable byline librarians have no way of knowing this "new" writer is one of his/her regulars, whose work would be ordered under other circumstances.

Having to become a new person every time another book is released is frustrating for any writer hoping to build a solid reputation among readers. It must be frustrating for editors who have put much thought and effort into acquiring and promoting the work of a writer whose work he/she admires.

And yet, for that new writer with a great first novel, this topsy-turvy method can be beneficial. A first novelist stands on exactly the same level, as far as the chain store buyer is concerned, with a seasoned writer with forty published books. Editors understand this, so theoretically it should be just a bit easier for that great first novel to gain a sympathetic reading.

Does this sound like a fantasy scenario that couldn't possibly be happening? It has happened to me, very recently, and my new agent tells me it must continue to happen until buying methods change.

High Mountain Winter, a novel of the Oregon Trail, was released one year as one of the spring lead titles by a major publisher. The byline was Frances Hurst. Although my pre-Columbian Indian novels sold very respectably, they were not lead titles and did not sell as they might have with the promotion given lead titles.

In other words, "the numbers" for the last of those would not be sufficient to cover the markets, nationwide, for a book promoted as a lead title. I could have insisted upon using my own name, but by so doing I would shoot my own book in the foot, so to speak.

So where will all this end? I wish I knew. Given the fact that publishing has become a sales-and-marketing-driven business, rather than a fairly profitable labor of love, as it began, there seems some likelihood that it will continue to descend into the realm of do-it-yourself books, endless series, and imitations of bestsellers.

There are alternatives, however. There is the potential for computer generated production and distribution of all sorts of books, bypassing the standard publishing route completely. There is also a growing number of small and university presses that produce high quality books in solid and sometimes impressive editions.

The secret of survival may lie in flexibility on the part of the writer. If one route is closed, there is usually another to be found. Our own bylines are important, but not all-important.

It is our books, our intellectual offspring, that are the principal concern. We want them to find homes with readers who will appreciate them. Whatever byline may appear on their covers, whatever format contains them, in one way or another we must strive to place them in good hands and do our best to see that they survive.

CHAPTER THIRTY-THREE

A FINAL WORD

Writing is a strange craft that demands the best we have inside us. It uses everything we have ever been or thought or seen or heard or read. It wrings us dry at its best, and at its worst it fills us with frustration and despair.

And yet...given the choice of being a writer or being anything else in the world, this is the craft I would choose.

With all its pitfalls and perversities, it can satisfy the soul as nothing else can ever hope to do.

INDEX

www.ingramcontent.com/pod-product-compliance
Lightning Source LLC
Chambersburg PA
CBHW030932090426
42737CB00007B/401